In Honor of the Bicentennial of the United States

The American Revolution: Three Views

The American Revolution: Three Views

Copyright 1975
American Brands, Inc.
New York

Acknowledgment

The three distinguished lectures
presented in this book
were selected from a series
sponsored by
the American Enterprise Institute
in celebration of
the Bicentennial of the United States.
American Brands, Inc.,
wishes to thank the Institute,
Irving Kristol, Martin Diamond,
and G. Warren Nutter
for their permission
to reprint these lectures

Contents

Foreword

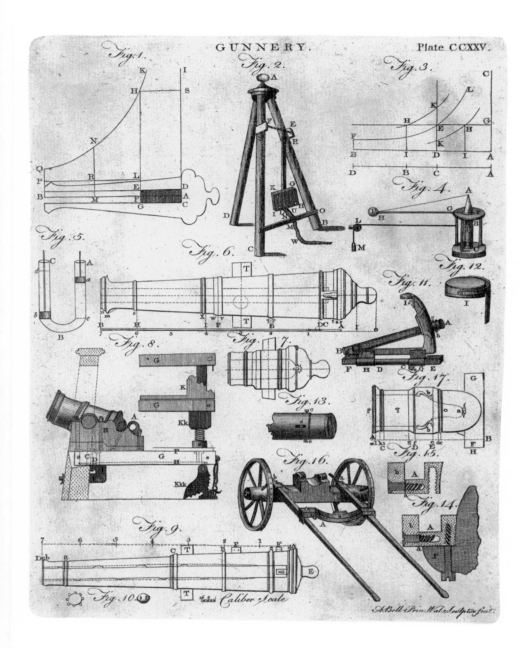

Caliber Scale

A.Bell. Prin. Wal. Sculptor fect.

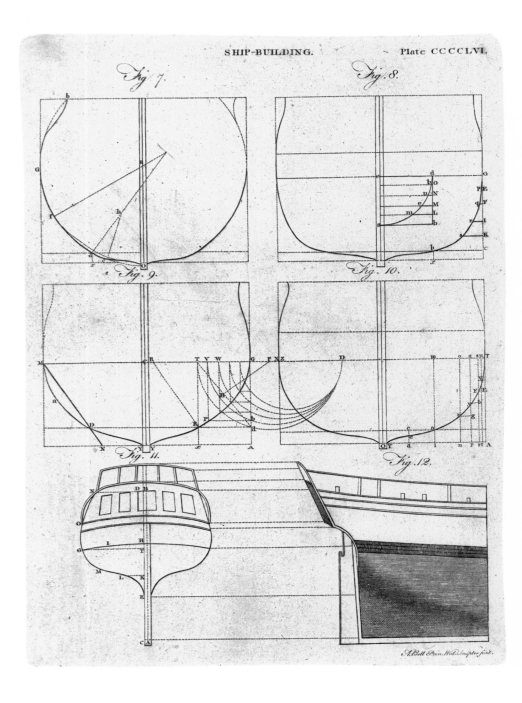

Fig. 7.
Fig. 8.
Fig. 9.
Fig. 10.
Fig. 11.
Fig. 12.

A. Bell Prin. Wal. Sculptor fecit.

Foreword

If it was "the blessings of liberty" for which the American colonists fought their revolution, the liberty they sought was economic liberty. Since 1607 the colonies had been trammeled in Britain's mercantilist system—sources of cheap raw material and taxes, consumers of British manufactured goods, denied freedom of manufacture and even freedom to trade abroad in their own commodities.

It is therefore not inappropriate for American Brands, Inc., a consumer goods company, to publish these views of the American Revolution to mark the nation's bicentennial. Our principal product, tobacco, was America's first industry, beginning with John Rolfe's first crop of exportable leaf grown in 1613. Another of our products, Bourbon, was distilled from tidewater corn only four years later. Freedom to produce commodities like these, to process and sell them in this country and abroad has made possible America's growth, supported its people, and reinforced the blessings of liberty during the two centuries of independence.

That is a rather deglamorized view of our cherished American Revolution. It is not romantic to think of economics or even "socioeconomics" as a first cause. Were the bluecoats at Valley Forge shivering and starving only for the freedom to trade with the West Indies without smuggling, or to win abstract freedom for a grateful posterity? The question answers itself. Unless they secured to themselves economic freedom, they would not have a grateful posterity, and perhaps no posterity at all. Thus Professor Diamond sees ours as "the revolution of sober expectations."

But sober expectations need not be ignoble ones, for as Professor Nutter points out, "To interpret the moving spirit of our founding years as nothing more than a craving for greater material comfort would be a travesty of history." Still, he adds,.."by the test of progress, freedom could hardly have been judged as a failure." But he too describes our forefathers' expectations as almost negatively sober:
"The documents of our Revolution protested against too much government, against the dead hand of paternalism and arbitrary power. Liberty to our Founders meant freedom from government."

Professor Kristol deals more with the "socio" than with the "economic" phase. He shows how the sober and specific objectives of our revolution were the very qualities that led to a constructive outcome. By contrast, he points out, revolutions of passionate expectation, aimed at liberty in the abstract, led to tumbrels, tyrants and off-battlefield savagery. (They still do.) If our revolution had been as passionate, as romantic, and as heroic as we now tend to color it, 1776 might also have ended up in animal savagery instead of leading to a new "political philosophy."

Adds Kristol: "A law-and-order revolution?
What kind of revolution is that, we ask ourselves?"
Perhaps a revolution that did not utterly reject the
values of the past but only structured a new
government to enhance them — perhaps that was
not so very revolutionary after all. Kristol's point
is that the nonexcessive nature of our revolution set
the stage for a free society.

We call the conflict that followed 1776 the War of
Independence. But the great outcome was not
independence from Britain *per se;* it was the fact that
this independence gave each American the freedom
to pursue the blessings of liberty in a new and
reasonably open society. And whatever rhetoric we
use for the political principle thus won — liberty,
independence, civil rights, freedom—all rests on an
economic base. It was no dislike of Britons or things
British which led the colonists to revolt. Most of the
colonists were transplanted Britons themselves; their
arts, their architecture, their dress and their language
were, and continued to be, British. At bottom it was
the harsh denial of economic freedom, expressed in
the stamp acts, the strict regulation of trade and the
prohibition of colonial manufacturing enterprise,
that created the breach. The revolution enabled the
colonists to be more free than English freemen
themselves. It uniquely avoided the out-of-hand,
emotional rejection of the past usually associated
with the word "revolution."

Across two centuries,
the American Revolution still speaks to us:

Professor Kristol:
The French Revolution promised —
as practically all revolutions have promised since —
the abolition of poverty.
The American Revolution promised no such thing...
the leaders of this revolution
understood what we today
have some difficulty in understanding:
namely, that poverty is abolished by economic growth,
not by economic redistribution —
there is never enough to distribute —
and that rebellions,
by creating instability and insecurity,
have mischievous consequences for economic growth.

Professor Diamond:
...the recent popular song
to the contrary notwithstanding,
the political pursuit of impossible dreams
leads to terror and tyranny
in the vain effort to actualize what cannot be.

Professor Nutter:
Wherever and however they acquired
their economic vision,
the makers of the Constitution
deliberately gave wide berth
to the economy of the nation being formed,
reserving only
a restrained guiding hand for government.

Today this has changed:..:"there is little in the
momentum of unfolding history," Nutter concludes,
"to comfort those who cherish freedom." But he ends
with a hope which every citizen of the United States
of America can cheer:

...having become so impressed with the fact
  that freedom is not everything or the only thing,
  perhaps we shall put
  that discovery behind us and comprehend,
  before it's too late,
  that without freedom all else is nothing.

American Brands is pleased to help disseminate the
views of three such distinguished thinkers as Messrs.
Kristol, Diamond, and Nutter. Each, in his own way,
is striking a blow for liberty. We hope this publication
will further that purpose — the purpose for which
the American republic was founded.

Robert K. Heimann
chairman and president
American Brands, Inc.
January 1975

The American Revolution: Three Views

The American Revolution As A Successful Revolution

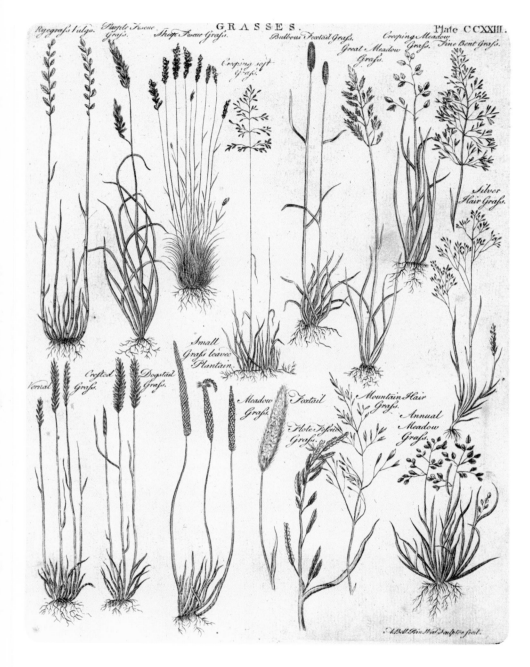

Ryegrass vulgo.   Purple Fescue   Sheep Fescue Grass.   Bulbous Foxtail Grass.   Creeping Meadow
                   Grass.   Grass.   Fine Bent Grass.

                                                                      Great Meadow
                                                                      Grass.

                              Creeping soft
                              grass.

                                                                                                      Silver
                                                                                                      Hair Grass.

                                              Small
                                              Grass leaves
                                              Plantain.

Vernal   Crested   Dogstail   Meadow   Foxtail   Mountain Hair
            Grass.   Grass.   Grass.   Grass.
                                                                                              Annual
                                                          Flote Fescue   Meadow
                                                          Grass.   Grass.

A. Bell Printal Sculptor fecit.

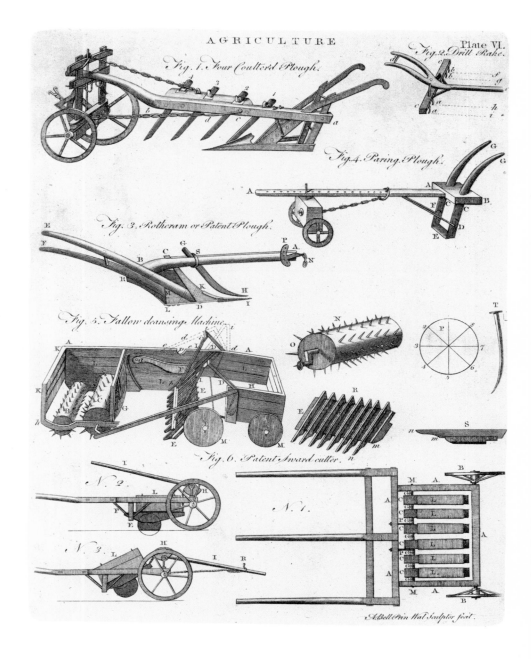

AGRICULTURE

Plate VI.

Fig. 1. Four Coulter'd Plough.

Fig. 2. Drill Rake.

Fig. 4. Paring Plough.

Fig. 3. Rotheram or Patent Plough.

Fig. 5. Fallow cleansing Machine.

Fig. 6. Patent Sward cutter.

N.º 2.

N.º 3.

N.º 1.

A. Bell & Brin Wal Sculptor fecit.

I
The American Revolution As A Successful Revolution
By Irving Kristol

I As we approach the bicentennial of the American
Revolution, we find ourselves in a paradoxical and
embarrassing situation. A celebration of some kind
certainly seems to be in order, but the urge to celebrate
is not exactly overwhelming. Though many will
doubtless ascribe this mood to various dispiriting
events of the recent past or to an acute public
consciousness of present problems, I think this would
be a superficial judgment. The truth is that, for
several decades now, there has been a noticeable loss
of popular interest in the Revolution, both as a
historical event and as a political symbol. The idea and
very word, "revolution," are in good repute today;
the American Revolution is not. We are willing enough,
on occasion, to pick up an isolated phrase from the
Declaration of Independence, or a fine declamation
from a Founding Father — Jefferson, usually — and use
these to point up the shortcomings of American
society as it now exists. Which is to say, we seem to be
prompt to declare that the Revolution was a success
only when it permits us to assert glibly that we have
subsequently failed it. But this easy exercise in
self-indictment, though useful in some respects,
is on the whole a callow affair.

23

It does not tell us, for instance, whether there is an important connection between that successful Revolution and our subsequent delinquencies. It merely uses the Revolution for rhetorical-political purposes, making no serious effort at either understanding it or understanding ourselves. One even gets the impression that many of us regard ourselves as too sophisticated to take the Revolution seriously — that we see it as one of those naïve events of our distant childhood which we have since long outgrown but which we are dutifully reminded of, at certain moments of commemoration, by insistent relatives who are less liberated from the past than we are.

I think I can make this point most emphatically by asking the simple question: what ever happened to George Washington? He used to be a Very Important Person — indeed, *the* most important person in our history. Our history books used to describe him, quite simply, as the "Father of his Country" and in the popular mind he was a larger-than-life figure to whom piety and reverence were naturally due. In the past fifty years, however, this figure has been radically diminished in size and virtually emptied of substance. In part, one supposes, this is because piety is a sentiment we seem less and less capable of, most especially piety toward fathers. We are arrogant and condescending toward all ancestors because we are so convinced we understand them better than they understood themselves — whereas piety assumes that they still understand us better than we understand ourselves. Reverence, too, is a sentiment which we, in our presumption, find somewhat unnatural.

Woodrow Wilson, like most Progressives of his time, complained about the "blind worship" of the Constitution by the American people. No such complaint is likely to be heard today. We debate whether or not we should obey the laws of the land, whereas for George Washington—and Lincoln too, who in his lifetime reasserted this point most eloquently—obedience to law was not enough: they thought that Americans, as citizens of a self-governing polity, ought to have *reverence* for their laws. Behind this belief, of course, was the premise that the collective wisdom incarnated in our laws, and especially in the fundamental law of the Constitution, understood us better than any one of us could ever hope to understand it. Having separated ourselves from our historic traditions and no longer recognizing the power inherent in tradition itself, we find this traditional point of view close to incomprehensible.

Equally incomprehensible to us is the idea that
George Washington was the central figure in a real,
honest-to-God revolution — the first significant
revolution of the modern era and one which can lay
claim to being the only truly successful revolution, on
a large scale, in the past two centuries. In his own
lifetime, no one doubted that he was the central
figure of that revolution. Subsequent generations did
not dispute the fact and our textbooks, until about a
quarter of a century ago, took it for granted, albeit
in an ever-more routine and unconvincing way.
We today, in contrast, find it hard to take George
Washington seriously as a successful revolutionary.
He just does not fit our conception of what a
revolutionary leader is supposed to be like. It is a
conception that easily encompasses Robespierre,
Lenin, Mao Tse-tung, or Fidel Castro — but can one
stretch it to include a gentleman (and a gentleman he
most certainly was) like George Washington? And so
we tend to escape from that dilemma by deciding that
what we call the American Revolution was not an
authentic revolution at all, but rather some kind of
pseudo-revolution, which is why it could be led by so
un-revolutionary a character as George Washington.

Hannah Arendt, in her very profound book
On Revolution, to which I am much indebted,
has written:

Revolutionary political thought
in the nineteenth and twentieth centuries has proceeded
as though there never had occurred
a revolution in the New World
and as though there never had been
any American notions and experiences
in the realm of politics and government
worth thinking about.

It is certainly indisputable that the world, when it contemplates the events of 1776 and after, is inclined to see the American Revolution as a French Revolution that never quite came off, whereas the Founding Fathers thought they had cause to regard the French Revolution as an American Revolution that had failed. Indeed, the differing estimates of these two revolutions are definitive of one's political philosophy in the modern world: there are two conflicting conceptions of politics, in relation to the human condition, which are symbolized by these two revolutions. There is no question that the French Revolution is, in some crucial sense, the more "modern" of the two. There is a question, however, as to whether this is a good or bad thing.

It is noteworthy that, up until about fifteen years ago, most American historians of this century tended to look at the American Revolution through non-American eyes. They saw it as essentially an abortive and incomplete revolution, in comparison with the French model. But more recently, historians have become much more respectful toward the American Revolution, and the work of Bernard Bailyn, Edmund S. Morgan, Caroline Robbins, Gordon S. Wood, and others is revealing to us once again what the Founding Fathers had, in their day, insisted was the case: that the American Revolution was an extremely *interesting* event, rich in implication for any serious student of politics. These historians have rediscovered for us the intellectual dimensions of the American Revolution, and it is fair to say that we are now in a position to appreciate just how extraordinarily self-conscious and reflective a revolution it was.

All revolutions unleash tides of passion, and the American Revolution was no exception. But it *was* exceptional in the degree to which it was able to subordinate these passions to serious and nuanced thinking about fundamental problems of political philosophy. The pamphlets, sermons, and newspaper essays of the revolutionary period — only now being reprinted and carefully studied — were extraordinarily "academic," in the best sense of that term. Which is to say, they were learned and thoughtful and generally sober in tone. This was a revolution infused by *mind* to a degree never approximated since, and perhaps never approximated before. By mind, not by dogma. The most fascinating aspect of the American Revolution is the severe way it kept questioning itself about the meaning of what it was doing. Enthusiasm there certainly was — a revolution is impossible without enthusiasm — but this enthusiasm was tempered by doubt, introspection, anxiety, skepticism. This may strike us as a very strange state of mind in which to make a revolution; and yet it is evidently the right state of mind for making a successful revolution. That we should have any difficulty in seeing this tells us something about the immaturity of our own political imagination, an immaturity not at all incompatible with what we take to be sophistication.

Just a few weeks ago, one of our most prominent statesmen remarked to an informal group of political scientists that he had been reading *The Federalist* papers and he was astonished to see how candidly our Founding Fathers could talk about the frailties of human nature and the necessity for a political system to take such frailties into account. It was not possible, he went on to observe, for anyone active in American politics today to speak publicly in this way: he would be accused of an imperfect democratic faith in the common man. Well, the Founding Fathers for the most part, and most of the time, subscribed to such an "imperfect" faith. They understood that republican self-government could not exist if humanity did not possess — at some moments, and to a fair degree — the traditional "republican virtues" of self-control, self-reliance, and a disinterested concern for the public good. They also understood that these virtues did not exist everywhere, at all times, and that there was no guarantee of their "natural" preponderance. James Madison put it this way:

As there is a degree of depravity in mankind
which requires a certain degree
of circumspection and distrust;
so there are other qualities in human nature
which justify a certain portion of esteem and confidence.
Republican government presupposes the existence
of these qualities in a higher degree
than any other form.

Despite the fact that Christian traditions are still strong in this country, it is hard to imagine any public figure casually admitting, as Madison did in his matter-of-fact way, that "there is a degree of depravity in mankind" which statesmen must take into account. We have become unaccustomed to such candid and unflattering talk about ourselves—which is, I suppose, only another way of saying that we now think democratic demagoguery to be the only proper rhetorical mode of address as between government and people in a republic. The idea, so familiar to the Puritans and still very much alive during our revolutionary era, that a community of individual sinners could, under certain special conditions, constitute a good community—just as a congregation of individual sinners could constitute a good church— is no longer entirely comprehensible to us.
We are therefore negligent about the complicated ways in which this transformation takes place and uncomprehending as to the constant, rigorous attentiveness necessary for it to take place at all.

The Founders thought that self-government was a chancy and demanding enterprise and that successful government in a republic was a most difficult business. We, in contrast, believe that republican self-government is an easy affair, that it need only be instituted for it to work on its own, and that when such government falters it must be as a consequence of personal incompetence or malfeasance by elected officials. Perhaps nothing reveals better than these different perspectives the intellectual distance we have traveled from the era of the Revolution. We like to think we have "progressed" along this distance. The approaching bicentennial is an appropriate occasion for us to contemplate the possibility that such "progress," should it continue, might yet be fatal to the American polity.

II   In what sense can the American Revolution be
     called a successful revolution? And if we agree that
     it was successful, why was it successful? These
     questions cannot be disentangled, the "that" and the
     "why" comprising together one's basic (if implicit)
     explanation of the term, "successful revolution."
     These questions are also anything but academic.
     Indeed I believe that, as one explores them, one finds
     oneself constrained to challenge a great many
     preconceptions, not only about the nature of
     revolution but about the nature of politics itself,
     which most of us today take for granted.

     To begin at the beginning: the American Revolution
     was successful in that those who led it were able, in
     later years, to look back in tranquillity at what they
     had wrought and to say that it was good. This was a
     revolution which, unlike all subsequent revolutions,
     did not devour its children: the men who made the
     revolution were the men who went on to create the
     new political order, who then held the highest elected
     positions in this order, and who all died in bed.

Not very romantic, perhaps. Indeed positively prosaic.
But it is this very prosaic quality of the American
Revolution that testifies to its success. It is the pathos
and poignancy of unsuccessful revolutions which
excite the poetic temperament; statesmanship which
successfully accomplishes its business is a subject
more fit for prose. Alone among the revolutions of
modernity, the American Revolution did not give rise
to the pathetic and poignant myth of "the revolution
betrayed." It spawned no literature of disillusionment;
it left behind no grand hopes frustrated, no grand
expectations unsatisfied, no grand illusions shattered.
Indeed, in one important respect the American
Revolution was so successful as to be almost
self-defeating: it turned the attention of thinking
men away from politics, which now seemed utterly
unproblematic, so that political theory lost its vigor,
and even the political thought of the Founding
Fathers was not seriously studied. This intellectual
sloth, engendered by success, rendered us
incompetent to explain this successful revolution to
the world, and even to ourselves. The American
political tradition became an inarticulate tradition:
it worked so well we did not bother to inquire why it
worked, and we are therefore intellectually disarmed
before those moments when it suddenly seems not
to be working so well after all.

The American Revolution was also successful in another important respect: it was a mild and relatively bloodless revolution. A war was fought, to be sure, and soldiers died in that war. But the rules of civilized warfare, as then established, were for the most part quite scrupulously observed by both sides: there was none of the butchery which we have come to accept as a natural concomitant of revolutionary warfare. More important, there was practically none of the off-battlefield savagery which we now assume to be inevitable in revolutions. There were no revolutionary tribunals dispensing "revolutionary justice"; there was no reign of terror; there were no bloodthirsty proclamations by the Continental Congress. Tories were dispossessed of their property, to be sure, and many were rudely hustled off into exile; but so far as I have been able to determine, not a single Tory was executed for harboring counter-revolutionary opinions. Nor, in the years after the Revolution, were Tories persecuted to any significant degree (at least by today's standards) or their children discriminated against at all. As Tocqueville later remarked, with only a little exaggeration, the Revolution "contracted no alliance with the turbulent passions of anarchy, but its course was marked, on the contrary, by a love of order and law."

A law-and-order revolution? What kind of revolution is that, we ask ourselves? To which many will reply that it could not have been much of a revolution after all—at best a shadow of the real thing, which is always turbulent and bloody and shattering of body and soul. Well, the American Revolution was not that kind of revolution at all, and the possibility we have to consider is that it was successful precisely because it was not that kind of revolution—that it is we rather than the American revolutionaries who have an erroneous conception of what a revolution is.

33

Dr. Arendt makes an important distinction between "rebellion" and "revolution." By her criteria the French and Russian revolutions should more properly be called "rebellions," whereas only the American Revolution is worthy of the name. A rebellion, in her terms, is a meta-political event, emerging out of a radical dissatisfaction with the human condition as experienced by the mass of the people, demanding instant "liberation" from this condition, an immediate transformation of all social and economic circumstance, a prompt achievement of an altogether "better life" in an altogether "better world." The spirit of rebellion is a spirit of desperation — a desperate rejection of whatever exists, a desperate aspiration toward some kind of utopia. A rebellion is more a sociological event than a political action. It is governed by a blind momentum which sweeps everything before it, and its so-called leaders are in fact its captives, and ultimately its victims. The modern world knows many such rebellions, and all end up as one version or another of "a revolution betrayed." The so-called "betrayal" is, in fact, nothing but the necessary conclusion of a rebellion. Since its impossible intentions are unrealizable and since its intense desperation will not be satisfied with anything less than impossible intentions, the end result is always a regime which pretends to embody these intentions and which enforces such false pretentions by terror.

A revolution, in contrast, is a political phenomenon. It aims to revise and reorder the political arrangements of a society, and is therefore the work of the political ego rather than of the political id. A revolution is a practical exercise in political philosophy, not an existential spasm of the social organism. It requires an attentive prudence, a careful calculation of means and ends, a spirit of sobriety— the kind of spirit exemplified by that calm, legalistic document, the Declaration of Independence.

All this is but another way of saying that a successful revolution cannot be governed by the spirit of the mob. Mobs and mob actions there will always be in a revolution, but if this revolution is not to degenerate into a rebellion, mob actions must be marginal to the central political drama. It may sound paradoxical but it nevertheless seems to be the case that only a self-disciplined people can dare undertake so radical a political enterprise as a revolution. This is almost like saying that a successful revolution must be accomplished by a people who want it but do not desperately need it—which was, indeed, the American condition in 1776. One may even put the case more strongly: a successful revolution is best accomplished by a people who do not really want it at all, but find themselves reluctantly making it. The American Revolution was exactly such a reluctant revolution.

The present-day student of revolutions will look in vain for any familiar kind of "revolutionary situation" in the American colonies prior to '76. The American people at that moment were the most prosperous in the world and lived under the freest institutions to be found anywhere in the world. They knew this well enough and boasted of it often enough. Their quarrel with the British crown was, in its origins, merely over the scope of colonial self-government, and hardly anyone saw any good reason why this quarrel should erupt into a war of independence. It was only after the war got under way that the American people decided that this was a good opportunity to make a revolution as well—that is, to establish a republican form of government.

Republican and quasi-republican traditions had always been powerful in the colonies, which were populated to such a large degree by religious dissenters who were sympathetic to the ideas incorporated in Cromwell's Commonwealth. Moreover, American political institutions from the very beginning were close to republican in fact, especially those of the Puritan communities of New England. Still, it is instructive to note that the word "republic" does not appear in the Declaration of Independence. Not that there was any real thought of reinstituting a monarchy in the New World: no one took such a prospect seriously. It was simply that, reluctant and cautious revolutionaries as they were, the Founding Fathers saw no need to press matters further than they had to, at that particular moment. To put it bluntly: they did not want events to get out of hand and saw no good reason to provoke more popular turbulence than was absolutely necessary.

One does not want to make the American Revolution an even more prosaic affair than it was. This was a revolution—a real one—and it was infused with a spirit of excitement and innovation. After all, what the American Revolution, once it got under way, was trying to do was no small thing. It was nothing less than the establishment, for the first time since ancient Rome, of a large republican nation, and the idea of reestablishing under modern conditions the glory that had been Rome's could hardly fail to be intoxicating. This Revolution did indeed have grand, even millenial, expectations as to the future role of this new nation in both the political imagination and political history of the human race. But certain things have to be said about these large expectations, if we are to see them in proper perspective.

The main thing to be said is that the millenarian tradition in America long antedates the Revolution and is not intertwined with the idea of revolution itself. It was the Pilgrim Fathers, not the Founding Fathers, who first announced that this was God's country, that the American people had a divine mission to accomplish, that this people had been "chosen" to create some kind of model community for the rest of mankind. This belief was already so firmly established by the time of the Revolution that it was part and parcel of our political orthodoxy, serving to legitimate an existing "American way of life" and most of the institutions associated with that way of life. It was a radical belief, in the sense of being bold and challenging and because this new "way of life" was so strikingly different from the lives that common people were then living in Europe. It was *not* a revolutionary belief. Crèvecoeur's famous paean of praise to "this new man, the American," was written well before the Revolution; and Crèvecoeur, in fact, opposed the American Revolution as foolish and unnecessary.

To this traditional millenarianism, the Revolution added the hope that the establishment of republican institutions would inaugurate a new and happier political era for all mankind. This hope was frequently expressed enthusiastically, in a kind of messianic rhetoric, but the men of the Revolution—most of them, most of the time—did not permit themselves to become bewitched by that rhetoric. Thus, though they certainly saw republicans as "the wave of the future," both Jefferson and Adams in the 1780s agreed that the French people were still too "depraved," as they so elegantly put it, to undertake an experiment in self-government. Self-government, as they understood it, presupposed a certain "way of life," and this in turn presupposed certain qualities on the part of the citizenry—qualities then designated as "republican virtues"—that would make self-government possible.

Similarly, though one can find a great many publicists during the Revolution who insisted that, with the severance of ties from Britain, the colonies had reverted to a Lockean "state of nature" and were now free to make a new beginning for all mankind and to create a new political order that would mark a new stage in human history—though such assertions were popular enough, it would be a mistake to take them too seriously. The fact is that Americans had encountered their "state of nature" generations earlier and had made their "social compact" at that time. The primordial American "social contract" was signed and sealed on the *Mayflower*—literally signed and sealed. The subsequent presence of all those signatures appended to the Declaration of Independence, beginning with John Hancock's, are but an echo of the original covenant.

To perceive the true purposes of the American Revolution, it is wise to ignore some of the more grandiloquent declamations of the moment — Tom Paine, an English radical who never really understood America, is especially worth ignoring — and to look at the kinds of political activity the Revolution unleashed. This activity took the form of constitution-making, above all. In the months and years immediately following the Declaration of Independence, all of our states drew up constitutions. These constitutions are terribly interesting in three respects. First, they involved relatively few basic changes in existing political institutions and almost no change at all in legal, social, or economic institutions; they were, for the most part, merely revisions of the preexisting charters. Secondly, most of the changes that were instituted had the evident aim of weakening the power of government, especially of the executive; it was these changes — and especially the strict separation of powers — that dismayed Turgot, Condorcet, and the other French *philosophes*, who understood revolution as an expression of the people's will-to-power rather than as an attempt to circumscribe political authority. Thirdly, in no case did any of these state constitutions tamper with the traditional system of local self-government. Indeed they could not, since it was this traditional system of local self-government which created and legitimized the constitutional conventions themselves.

In short, the Revolution reshaped our political institutions in such a way as to make them more responsive to popular opinion and less capable of encroaching upon the personal liberties of the citizen — liberties which long antedated the new constitutions and which in no way could be regarded as the creation or consequence of revolution.

Which is to say that the purpose of this Revolution was to bring our political institutions into a more perfect correspondence with an actual "American way of life" which no one even dreamed of challenging. This "restructuring," as we would now call it — because it put the possibility of republican self-government once again on the political agenda of Western civilization — was terribly exciting to Europeans as well as Americans. But for the Americans involved in this historic task, it was also terribly frightening. It is fair to say that no other revolution in modern history made such relatively modest innovations with such an acute sense of anxiety. The Founding Fathers were well aware that if republicanism over the centuries had become such a rare form of government, there must be good reasons for it. Republican government, they realized, must be an exceedingly difficult regime to maintain — that is, it must have grave inherent problems. And so they were constantly scurrying to their libraries, ransacking classical and contemporary political authors, trying to discover why republics fail, and endeavoring to construct a "new political science" relevant to American conditions which would give this new republic a fair chance of succeeding. That "new political science" was eventually to be embodied in *The Federalist* — the only original work of political theory ever produced by a revolution and composed by successful revolutionaries. And the fact that very few of us have ever felt the need seriously to study *The Federalist* and that Europeans — or in our own day, Asians and Africans — have barely heard of it tells us how inadequately we understand the American Revolution, and how distant the real American Revolution has become from the idea of revolution by which we moderns are now possessed.

This idea of revolution as the world understands it today, is what Dr. Arendt calls "rebellion." It involves a passionate rejection of the status quo — its institutions and the way of life associated with these institutions. It rejects everything that exists because it wishes to create everything anew—a new social order, a new set of economic arrangements, a new political entity, a new kind of human being. It aims to solve not merely the political problem of the particular political community, at that particular moment, but every other problem that vexes humanity. Its spirit is the spirit of undiluted, enthusiastic, free-floating messianism: it will be satisfied with nothing less than a radical transformation of the human condition. It is an idea and a movement which is both meta-political and sub-political—above and below politics—because it finds the political realm itself too confining for its ambitions. Meta-politically, it is essentially a religious phenomenon, seized with the perennial promise of redemption. Sub-politically, it is an expression of the modern technological mentality, confident of its power to control and direct all human processes as we have learned to control and direct the processes of nature. Inevitably, its swollen pride and fanatical temper lead to tragic failure. But precisely because of this pride and this fanaticism, failure leads only to partial and temporary disillusionment. When this kind of revolution gets "betrayed"—which is to say, when the consequences of revolution lose all congruence with its original purpose—the true revolutionary believer will still look forward to a second coming of the authentic and unbetrayable revolution.

The French Revolution was the kind of modern revolution I have been describing; the American Revolution was not. It is because of this, one supposes, that the French Revolution has captured the imagination of other peoples—has become indeed the model of "real" revolution—in a way that the American Revolution has not been able to do. The French Revolution promised not only a reformation of France's political institutions, but far more than that. It promised, for instance—as practically all revolutions have promised since—the abolition of poverty. The American Revolution promised no such thing, in part because poverty was not such a troublesome issue in this country, but also—one is certain—because the leaders of this revolution understood what their contemporary, Adam Smith, understood and what we today have some difficulty in understanding: namely, that poverty is abolished by economic growth, not by economic redistribution— there is never enough to distribute—and that rebellions, by creating instability and uncertainty, have mischievous consequences for economic growth. Similarly, the French Revolution promised a condition of "happiness" to its citizens under the new regime, whereas the American Revolution promised merely to permit the individual to engage in the "pursuit of happiness."

It should not be surprising, therefore, that in the war of ideologies which has engulfed the twentieth century, the United States is at a disadvantage. This disadvantage does not flow from any weakness on our part. It is not, as some say, because we have forgotten our revolutionary heritage and therefore have nothing to say to a discontented and turbulent world. We have, indeed, much to say, only it is not what our contemporaries want to hear. It is not even what we ourselves want to hear, and in *that* sense it may be correct to claim we have forgotten our revolutionary heritage. Our revolutionary message—which is a message not of the Revolution itself but of the American political tradition from the *Mayflower* to the Declaration of Independence to the Constitution—is that a self-disciplined people *can* create a political community in which an ordered liberty will promote both economic prosperity and political participation. To the teeming masses of other nations, the American political tradition says: to enjoy the fruits of self-government, you must first cease being "masses" and become a "people," attached to a common way of life, sharing common values, and existing in a condition of mutual trust and sympathy as between individuals and even social classes. It is a distinctly odd kind of "revolutionary" message, by twentieth century criteria—so odd that it seems not revolutionary at all, and yet so revolutionary that it seems utterly utopian. What the twentieth century wants to hear is the grand things that a new government will do for the people who put their trust in it. What the American political tradition says is that the major function of government is, in Professor Oakeshott's phrase, to "tend to the arrangements of society," and that free people do not make a covenant or social contract with their government, or with the leaders of any "movement," but among themselves.

In the end, what informs the American political tradition is a proposition and a premise. The proposition is that the best national government is, to use a phrase the Founding Fathers were fond of, "mild government." The premise is that you can only achieve "mild government" if you have a solid bedrock of local self-government, so that the responsibilities of national government are limited in scope. And a corollary of this premise is that such a bedrock of local self-government can only be achieved by a people who—through the shaping influence of religion, education, and their own daily experience—are capable of governing themselves in those small and petty matters which are the stuff of local politics.

Does this conception of politics have any relevance to the conditions in which people live today in large areas of the world—the so-called underdeveloped areas, especially? We are inclined, I think, to answer instinctively in the negative, but that answer may itself be a modern ideological prejudice. We take it for granted that if a people live in comparative poverty, they are necessarily incapable of the kind of self-discipline and sobriety that makes for effective self-government in their particular communities. Mind you, I am not talking about starving people, who are in a prepolitical condition and whose problem is to get a strong and effective government of almost any kind. I am talking about *comparatively* poor people. And our current low estimate of the political capabilities of such people is an ideological assumption, not an objective fact. Many of our frontier communities, at the time of the Revolution and for decades afterwards, were poor by any standards. Yet this poverty was not, for the most part, inconsistent with active self-government. There have been communities in Europe, too, which were very poor— not actually starving, of course, but simply very poor— yet were authentic political communities. The popular musical, *Fiddler on the Roof,* gave us a picture of such a community. It is always better not to be so poor, but poverty need not be a pathological condition, and political pathology is not an inevitable consequence of poverty, just as political pathology is not inevitably abolished by prosperity. Poor people can cope with their poverty in many different ways. They are people, not sociological creatures and in the end they will cope as their moral and political convictions tell them to cope. These convictions, in turn, will be formed by the expectations that their community addresses to them—expectations which they freely convert into obligations.

In *The Brothers Karamazov,* Dostoevsky says that the spirit of the Antichrist, in its modern incarnation, will flaunt the banner, "First feed people, and *then* ask of them virtue." This has, in an amended form, indeed become the cardinal and utterly conventional thesis of modern politics. The amended form reads: "First make people prosperous, and then ask of them virtue." Whatever reservations one might have about Dostoevsky's original thesis, this revised version is, in the perspective of the Judaeo-Christian tradition, unquestionably a blasphemy. It is also, in the perspective of the American political tradition, a malicious and inherently self-defeating doctrine — self-defeating because those who proclaim it obviously have lost all sense of what virtue, religious or political, means. Nevertheless, practically all of us today find it an inherently plausible doctrine, a staple of our political discourse. This being the case, it is only natural that we ourselves should have such difficulty understanding the American political tradition, and that when we expend it to the world, we distort it in all sorts of ways which will make it more palatable to the prejudices of the modern political mentality.

III   It would not be fair to conclude that the American political tradition is flawless, and that it is only we, its heirs, who are to blame for the many problems our society is grappling with—and so ineptly. The American Revolution was a successful revolution, but there is no such thing, either in one's personal life or in a nation's history, as unambiguous success. The legacy of the American Revolution and of the entire political tradition associated with it is problematic in all sorts of ways. Strangely enough, we have such an imperfect understanding of this tradition that, even as we vulgarize it or question it or disregard it, we rarely address ourselves to its problematic quality.

The major problematic aspect of this tradition has to do with the relationship of the "citizen" to the "common man." And the difficulties we have in defining this relationship are best illustrated by the fact that, though we have been a representative democracy for two centuries now, we have never developed an adequate theory of representation.

More precisely we have developed *two* contradictory
theories of representation, both of which can claim
legitimacy within the American political tradition and
both of which were enunciated, often by the same
people, during the Revolution. The one sees the public
official as a "common man" who has a mandate to
reflect the opinions of the majority; the other sees the
public official as a somewhat uncommon man—a
more-than-common man, if you will—who, because of
his talents and character, is able to take a larger view
of the "public interest" than the voters who elected
him or the voters who failed to defeat him. One might
say that the first is a "democratic" view of the legislator,
the second a "republican" view. The American political
tradition has always had a kind of double vision
on this whole problem, which in turn makes for a
bewildering moral confusion. Half the time we
regard our politicians as, in the nature of things,
probably corrupt and certainly untrustworthy; the
other half of the time, we denounce them for failing
to be models of integrity and rectitude. Indeed,
we have a profession—journalism—which seems
committed to both of these contradictory propositions.
But politicians are pretty much like the rest of us and
tend to become the kinds of people they are expected
to be. The absence of clear and distinct expectations
has meant that public morality in this country has
never been, and is not, anything we can be proud of.

In a way, the ambiguity in our theory of representation points to a much deeper ambiguity in that system of self-government which emerged from the Revolution and the Constitutional Convention. That system has been perceptively titled, by Professor Martin Diamond, "a democratic republic." Now, we tend to think of these terms as near-synonyms, but in fact they differ significantly in their political connotations. Just how significant the difference is becomes clear if we realize that the America which emerged from the Revolution and the Constitutional Convention was the first democratic republic in history. The political philosophers of that time could study the history of republics and they could study the history of democracies, but there was no opportunity for them to study both together. When the Founding Fathers declared that they had devised a new kind of political entity based on "a new science of politics," they were not vainly boasting or deceiving themselves. It is we, their political descendants, who tend to be unaware of the novelty of the American political enterprise, and of the risks and ambiguities inherent in that novelty. We simplify and vulgarize and distort, because we have lost the sense of how bold and innovative the Founding Fathers were, and of how problematic — necessarily problematic — is the system of government, and the society, which they established. Witness the fact that, incredibly enough, at our major universities it is almost impossible to find a course, graduate or undergraduate, devoted to *The Federalist*.

What is the difference between a "democracy" and a "republic"? In a democracy, the will of the people is supreme. In a republic, it is not the will of the people but the rational consensus of the people—a rational consensus which is implicit in the term "consent"— which governs the people. That is to say, in a democracy, popular passion may rule—*may*, though it need not—but in a republic, popular passion is regarded as unfit to rule, and precautions are taken to see that it is subdued rather than sovereign. In a democracy all politicians are, to some degree, demagogues: they appeal to people's prejudices and passions, they incite their expectations by making reckless promises, they endeavor to ingratiate themselves with the electorate in every possible way. In a republic, there are not supposed to be such politicians, only statesmen—sober, unglamorous, thoughtful men who are engaged in a kind of perpetual conversation with the citizenry. In a republic, a fair degree of equality and prosperity are important goals, but it is liberty that is given priority as the proper end of government. In a democracy, these priorities are reversed: the status of men and women as consumers of economic goods is taken to be more significant than their status as participants in the creation of political goods. A republic is what we would call "moralistic" in its approach to both public and private affairs; a democracy is more easygoing, more "permissive" as we now say, even more cynical.

The Founding Fathers perceived that their new nation was too large, too heterogeneous, too dynamic, too mobile for it to govern itself successfully along strict republican principles. And they had no desire at all to see it governed along strict democratic principles, since they did not have that much faith in the kinds of "common men" likely to be produced by such a nation. So they created a new form of "popular government," to use one of their favorite terms, that incorporated both republican and democratic principles, in a complicated and ingenious way. This system has lasted for two centuries, which means it has worked very well indeed. But in the course of that time, we have progressively forgotten what kind of system it is and *why* it works as well as it does. Every now and then, for instance, we furiously debate the question of whether or not the Supreme Court is meeting its obligations as a democratic institution. The question reveals a startling ignorance of our political tradition. The Supreme Court is not—and was never supposed to be—a democratic institution; it is a republican institution which counterbalances the activities of our various democratic institutions. Yet I have discovered that when you say this to college students, they do not understand the distinction and even have difficulty thinking about it.

So it would seem that today, two hundred years after the American Revolution, we are in a sense victims of its success. The political tradition out of which it issued and the political order it helped to create are imperfectly comprehended by us. What is worse, we are not fully aware of this imperfect comprehension and are frequently smug in our convenient misunderstandings. The American Revolution certainly merits celebration. But it would be reassuring if a part of that celebration were to consist, not merely of pious clichés, but of a serious and sustained effort to achieve a deeper and more widespread understanding of just what it is we are celebrating.

The American Revolution: Three Views

The Revolution Of Sober Expectations

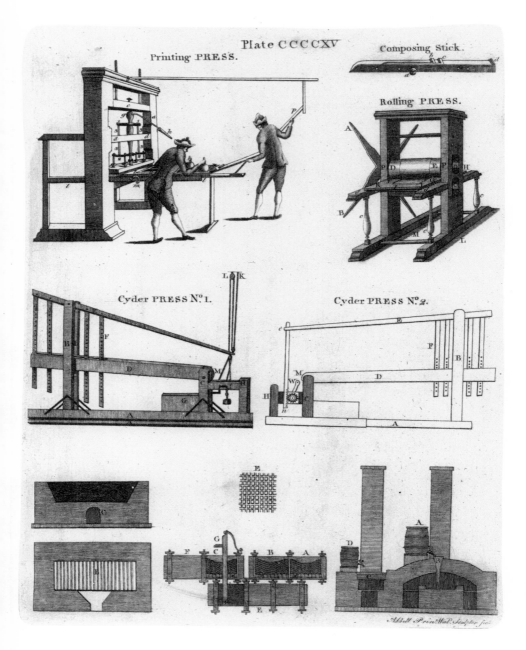

Plate CCCCXV

Printing PRESS.

Composing Stick.

Rolling PRESS.

Cyder PRESS No. 1.

Cyder PRESS No. 2.

Abbott Print Wal. Sculptor fec.

Plate CCLXXXVI.

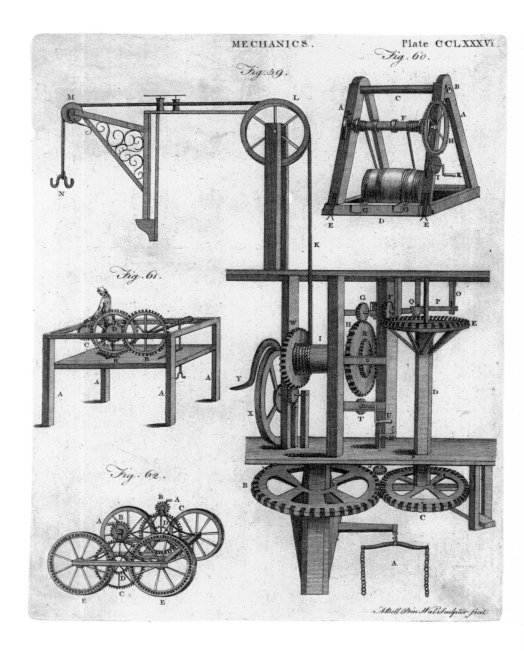

Fig. 59.

Fig. 60.

Fig. 61.

Fig. 62.

A.Bell Prin.Wal.Sculptor fecit.

II
The Revolution
Of Sober Expectations
By Martin Diamond

I   "I am filled with deep emotion at finding myself
standing here in the place where were collected
together the wisdom, the patriotism, the devotion to
principle, from which sprang the institutions under
which we live."[1] Those lovely words, I am sorry to say,
are not my own. They were uttered by Abraham
Lincoln in February 1861, only days before he assumed
the terrible burdens of his presidency. But I cannot
possibly find words better to express my own
deep emotion at having the opportunity to share with
you, in this hallowed place, my reflections as these
are occasioned by the impending bicentennial of
our national birth.

Because of the struggle then tormenting and dividing
the Union, Lincoln was obliged to look back upon the
origins of the American republic to find the wisdom,
patriotism, and devotion to principle that might save
the Union and reinspirit its republican institutions.
We are under no such compelling necessity tonight.
Our occasion is only inspired by the happy imminence
of our bicentennial. And yet, for us too the backward
glance remains a necessity.

Lincoln was obliged to look back to the men who met in Independence Hall in 1776 because it was their thoughts and words expressed immortally in the Declaration of Independence "from which sprang the institutions under which we live." We live still to an amazing extent under those same institutions. And like Lincoln, if we wish to understand those institutions, then we too must return to the thoughts of the Founding Fathers. We too must look to the architects for the plan of the house in which we still reside. No task could be more agreeable to me here, the child of immigrant grandparents whose grateful patriotism instructed my youth.

There is a fascinating ambiguity in those words of Lincoln which I have quoted. We must remember that there were two great happenings here at Independence Square, the first in 1776 when independence was proclaimed in the Declaration, and the second eleven years later when the Federal Convention met for four long months and drafted the Constitution. When we look back to our origins we look to the same place, here in Philadelphia, but to two different times and events — to 1776 and 1787, to the Declaration and the Constitution. They are the two springs of our existence. To understand their relationship is to understand the political core of our being, and hence to understand what it is that we are soon to celebrate the bicentennial of. It is to this never-to-be-severed relationship of the Declaration and the Constitution that I address my remarks.

In doing so I simply follow the lead of Lincoln. Let me repeat his words.

I am filled with deep emotion
at finding myself standing here in the place
where were collected together
the wisdom, the patriotism, the devotion to principle,
from which sprang the institutions
under which we live.

Notice how neatly Lincoln blends in this single sentence both 1776 and 1787, both Declaration and Constitution. By the "institutions under which we live," he refers of course to the institutions devised by the framers of the Constitution. But these institutions, Lincoln reminds us in the same breath, sprang from a "devotion to principle," to the principle of the Declaration. Only in the unity of the Declaration's principle and the Constitution's institutions does the American Republic achieve its complete being, and Lincoln never ceased from the effort to sustain or restore that unity. We must do no less.

II What wants understanding is precisely how our institutions of government sprang from the principle of the Declaration of Independence. How and to what extent were they generated by the Declaration of Independence? And what more had to be added actually to frame those institutions? We find a clue further on in Lincoln's speech — his "wholly unprepared speech," it is humbling and yet inspiring to note.

All the political sentiments I entertain
have been drawn,
so far as I have been able to draw them,
from the sentiments which originated,
and were given to the world
from this hall in which we stand.
I have never had a feeling politically
that did not spring from the sentiments
embodied in the Declaration of Independence?

Now this sentiment that Lincoln drew from the Declaration was that document's passionate devotion to the principle of liberty.

...something in that Declaration giving liberty,
not alone to the people of this country,
but hope to the world for all future time.
It was that which gave promise
that in due time the weights should be lifted
from the shoulders of all men,
and that all should have an equal chance.
This is the sentiment embodied
in that Declaration of Independence.

We must take careful heed of Lincoln's remarkable stress, throughout this speech from which we are quoting, on the words feeling and sentiment. He carefully limits his indebtedness to the Declaration only to certain sentiments and feelings, that is, to the spirit of liberty within which he conceives American government and its institutions. Indeed, he could not have done otherwise, for there is nothing in the Declaration which goes beyond that sentiment of liberty. As we shall see, noble document that the Declaration is, indispensable source of the feelings and sentiments of Americans and of the spirit of liberty in which their institutions were conceived, the Declaration is devoid of guidance as to what those institutions should be.

In addition to inferring this from Lincoln's speech, we have also the highest possible authority for this conclusion: namely, the testimony of the "Father of the Constitution," James Madison, and the acceptance of that testimony by the author of the Declaration, Thomas Jefferson. In 1825 the two patriarchs of the American founding engaged in a correspondence regarding a possible required reading list for students at the Law School of the University of Virginia. They took for granted, as Madison said, that the students should be required to read books that would inculcate "the true doctrines of liberty" which are "exemplified in our political system."[3] But it is not easy, Madison wrote, to find books that will be both "guides and guards" for the purpose. The work of John Locke, for example, Madison went on, was "admirably calculated to impress on young minds the right of nations to establish their own governments and to inspire a love of free ones." (This "love" would seem to be exactly what Lincoln meant by the "sentiment" of the Declaration.) But Locke could not teach those future lawyers how to protect "our Republican charters," that is, how to protect the American federal and state constitutions from being corrupted by false interpretations, because Locke gave insufficient guidance regarding the nature of our republican institutions.

Now to put these words in a letter to Jefferson, who, as the author of the Declaration, had clearly drawn inspiration from John Locke, would seem to be cutting pretty close to the bone. But Madison had no reason to hesitate in thus writing to his old friend because he could count on Jefferson's calmly agreeing with his view. Indeed, he proceeded to make his point even more explicitly. "The Declaration of Independence," Madison continued, "though rich in fundamental principles, and saying everything that could be said in the same number of words"— it never hurts to be gentle with an author's pride no matter how close a friend he is —"falls nearly under a like observation." What his careful eighteenth century language is saying is plainly this: The principles of Locke and of Jefferson's Declaration are infinitely valuable for inspiring in young minds a proper love of free government; but that is all that those principles reach to. The Declaration, Madison is saying and Jefferson cheerfully agrees, offers no guidance for the construction of free government and hence offers no aid in protecting the American form of free government under the Constitution. For that purpose, Madison does not scruple to add, one must turn to *The Federalist* "as the most authentic exposition of the text of the federal Constitution." In short, the patriarchs Jefferson and Madison agree with Lincoln, as I have interpreted him, in their understanding of the noble but limited work of the Declaration. The American founding, as we shall see, is only begun by the Declaration. It reaches its completion with the Constitution.

But civilly pious as we ought to be tonight, we need
not let the argument I am making rest with the
splendid authority of Lincoln, Madison, and Jefferson.
We may sustain their judgment by our independent
reading of the text of the Declaration. The relevant
passage is the one usually printed as the second
paragraph, the passage dealing with the truths the
Declaration holds to be self-evident. Now this does
not, by the way, mean evident to everyone, as it has
come to be thought in these disbelieving relativistic
days. The mockers say—Those truths aren't evident
to me; I'm into a different bag, and since they aren't
evident to me they cannot truly be truths. The author
of the Declaration knew that these truths would not
be self-evident to kings and nobles, not to predeter-
mined adversaries, nor to anyone of insufficient or
defective vision. Indeed Jefferson knew that those
truths had not hitherto been held as evident by the
vast majority of mankind. But, by self-evidence,
the Declaration does not refer to the selves to whom
the truths are evident, but rather means that the
evidentness of the truths is contained within the
truths themselves. That is, these truths are not to be
reached at the end of a chain of reasoning; they are
not the fruit of supporting evidence, inference, and
argument; but rather, carrying the evidence of their
truthfulness within themselves, their truth is to be
grasped by a kind of direct seeing or perception.
And, we may add, their truthfulness was to be
vindicated by the excellence of their consequences.
It would be by means of triumphant freedom that
others would be led in time also to see and then to
hold those truths to be self-evident. It was up to the
American Revolution and the future American
regime to vindicate them.

The Declaration holds certain truths to be self-evident: that all men are created equal, that they are endowed by their Creator with certain unalienable rights among which are life, liberty, and the pursuit of happiness, that governments, whose proper end is to secure these rights, may only be instituted by the consent of the governed, and that, when government becomes destructive of those rights, the people have the further right to alter or abolish it and reinstitute another in its place. Now these truths do not rise by inference one from the other, but are each equally and independently self-evident; and each is indispensably a part of a whole that forms the "sentiment" of the Declaration. Yet for our purpose tonight, and perhaps even intrinsically, we may single out as the most important political truth the comprehensive one regarding the institution of government, namely, that government exists to secure unalienable rights and must be instituted by popular consent. Intrinsically, this truth may be the most important because the other truths become political only in relation to it, or are ancillary to it. Thus men are created equal but only with respect to the equal possession of certain unalienable rights. Those rights give the content to and hence define our equality: what we are equally is equally free. But this equal freedom becomes, of course, political freedom, and hence politically interesting only under government. And, the final self-evident truth, that is, the right to overthrow despotic government and reinstitute a new one, is obviously ancillary to the truth that deals with what legitimate government is and must do.

What is especially interesting to us tonight is the way this political truth of the Declaration has been transformed as it formed and then was absorbed into the historical American credo of government.

We must read the Declaration closely to free ourselves from two centuries of obscuring usage. We have transformed the Declaration in our minds by reading the phrase "consent of the governed" as meaning rule by majorities, that is, democratic government. Indeed we think of the Declaration as our great democratic document, as the clarion call to and the guide to our democratic nature. But the Declaration does *not* say that consent is the means by which government is to operate. Rather, it says that consent is necessary only to institute the government, that is, to establish it.

The people need not, then, *establish* a government which *operates* by means of their consent. In fact, the Declaration says that they may organize government on "such principles" as they choose, and they may choose "any form of government" they deem appropriate to secure their rights. That is, the Declaration was not prescribing any particular form of government at all, but rather was following John Locke's contract theory, which taught the right of the people, in seeking to secure their liberties, to establish *any* form of government. And by any form of government the Declaration emphatically includes — as any literate eighteenth century reader would have understood — not only the democratic form of government but also aristocratic and monarchical government as well. That is why, for example, the Declaration has to submit facts to a "candid world" to prove the British king guilty of a "long train of abuses." Tom Paine, by way of contrast, could dispose of King George more simply. Paine deemed George III unfit to rule simply because he was a *king* and kingly rule was illegitimate as such. The fact that George was a "Royal Brute" was only frosting on the cake; for Paine his being royal was sufficient warrant for deposing him. But the Declaration, on the contrary, is obliged to prove that George was indeed a brute. That is, the Declaration holds George III "unfit to be the ruler of a free people" not because he was a king, but because he was a *tyrannical* king. Had the British monarchy continued to secure to the colonists their rights, as it had prior to the long train of abuses, the colonists would not have been entitled to rebel. It was only the fact, according to the Declaration, that George had become a tyrannical king that supplied the warrant for revolution.

Thus the Declaration, strictly speaking, is neutral on the question of forms of government: *any* form is legitimate provided it secures equal freedom and is instituted by popular consent. But from this it follows that the Declaration, while richly nurturing in humanity a love of free government and thus supplying Lincoln with all his political sentiments, can offer no guidance whatsoever, as Madison said, for the American democratic institutions which sprang from that love of freedom. That guidance is to be found in the thought which shaped the Constitution and is to be found in the Constitution itself which framed the institutions under which we live. It is to the Constitution that we must ultimately turn as the completion of the American Revolution. As to those democratic institutions, the Declaration says no more than this: If you choose the democratic form of government, rather than the aristocratic or monarchic or any mixture thereof, it must be a democratic government which secures to all people their unalienable rights. But how to do that? The Declaration is silent.

III   Indeed this silence is the splendid distinction of the American Revolution. And it is the first evidence of the sobriety to which I allude in the title of this lecture, "The Revolution of Sober Expectations." The Revolution was, so to speak, only half a revolution. It *did* overthrow a government, albeit a distant one; it did in a revolutionary way abolish an existing government — and that is at least half a revolution — but it did not in the same breath commit itself to the shape of the new government to be instituted.

The makers of the American Revolution did not think themselves in possession of the simple and complete political truth, capable of instant application as a panacea for government. They claimed possession of only half the truth, namely, the self-evident truth that equal freedom must be the foundation of all political society. And in the name of that equal freedom they made half a revolution. But, soberly and moderately, they left open the question of institutions of government.

These they knew would have to be forged from old materials, perhaps worked and reworked, and with a cool awareness that the new American institutions would be subject still to perennial human frailty and folly. The Declaration, then, limited the dangerous passions of revolution only to the unmaking of a tyrannical government. It gave no license to new rulers to carry those revolutionary passions directly into the making of new government. That making of new government would have to find its way through still uncharted paths to be trod soberly and prudently.

But what have I left, it may be asked, of our once glorious Declaration? I have argued, as emphatically as I can, that the Declaration soberly left open the question of forms of government and its institutions. And in so doing I have perhaps reduced its claims and its reach, *as these are now understood.* But after the French and Russian revolutions we have a utopianly grandiloquent idea of revolution, a different idea of revolution from that of the American revolutionaries. I do not believe that Jefferson and his colleagues, or that Madison or Lincoln, would have understood the Declaration otherwise than I have stated it; nor would they think me to have diminished it. From our perspective it may look like only half a revolution, but they understood that that was nonetheless revolution indeed and revolution enough. What was truly revolutionary in the American Revolution and its Declaration of Independence was that liberty, civil liberty — the doctrine of certain unalienable rights — was made the end of government. Not, as had been the case for millennia, whatever end power haphazardly imposed upon government; nor any longer the familiar variety of ends — not virtue, not piety, not privilege or wealth, not merely protection, and not empire and dominion; but now deliberately the principle of liberty.

It was this that led Lincoln to offer "All honor to Jefferson — to the man who, in the concrete pressure of a struggle for national independence by a single people, had the coolness, forecast, and capacity to introduce into a merely revolutionary document, an abstract truth, applicable to all men and all times."[4] A "merely revolutionary document" would have demanded a mere revolving — such was the traditional meaning of the word revolution — of power from one set of hands to another, from the few to the many or the many to the few; but the Declaration instead pledged the American Revolution to an abstract principle, to the "definitions and axioms of free society." For the same reason as Lincoln and in the same spirit, Madison likewise praised the "leaders of the Revolution" for accomplishing a "revolution which has no parallel in the annals of human society."[5]

The events that culminated in revolution began modestly in 1763 when, in response to new British imperial measures, the colonists sought to assert the traditional English liberties they had enjoyed during a century and a half of "salutary neglect." In this they were little different from Englishmen before them who had fought their battles in the name of ancient privileges and feudal immunities and time-honored customs. But gradually the issue subtly changed, and the abstract idea of liberty came to overlay the appeal to traditional and concrete English liberties. In the course of the intensifying struggle, the Americans gradually came to see those traditional English liberties, not as a growth merely peculiar to English soil and custom, but as having happily embodied the abstract principle of civil liberty as this had been stated, for example, by Locke and Montesquieu. What Montesquieu did as a deliberate work of political theory, the Americans enacted in the course of a political struggle: Each transformed concrete English liberties into the universal principle of liberty. And, finally, rejecting English rule as now hopelessly despotic, America launched its Revolution simply and expressly upon the principle of liberty. Thus Lord Acton dramatically, but not implausibly, concluded that "In the strictest sense the history of liberty dated from 1776 'for never till then had men sought liberty knowing what they sought.'"[6]

This was the heady stuff of the American Revolution. But still in its very dedication to the abstract principle of liberty, which made the American Revolution authentically revolutionary, was contained also the second element of that sobriety which made it a "revolution of sober expectations." While modern followers of Edmund Burke may warn of the dangers of devotion to abstract principles, they cannot blink aside the revolutionary American devotion to precisely such an abstract principle. The American truth was undeniably as abstract as, say, Robespierre's tyrannizing truth or Lenin's tyrannizing truth.

And yet there is indeed something moderate and nonutopian in the American devotion to liberty which warrants Burkean celebration. Whence then the difference? Wherein was the American Revolution one of sober expectations while the Jacobin and Leninist were revolutions of unbridled expectations? The answer lies not in degrees of devotion to abstractness, but in the substantive nature of the principle each was abstractly devoted to. It is one thing to be abstractly devoted to the Reign of Virtue or to unlimited equality in all respects or to mass fraternity or to classless society or to the transformation of the human condition itself, and quite another to be devoted to the abstract principle of civil liberty. Civil liberty as a goal constrains its followers to moderation, legality, and rootedness in regular institutions. Morever, moderate civil liberty does not require terror and tyranny for its fulfillment. Liberty is an abstract principle capable of achievement; Jacobin or Leninist equality or mass fraternity are not. Moderate civil liberty is a possible dream, utopian equality and fraternity are impossible dreams. And the recent popular song to the contrary notwithstanding, the political pursuit of impossible dreams leads to terror and tyranny in the vain effort to actualize what cannot be.

73

The revolution in America, Tocqueville said,

...was caused by a mature and thoughtful taste
  for freedom
  not by some vague, undefined instinct
  for independence
  (that is, for absence of order and constraint).
  No disorderly passions drove it on;
  on the contrary,
  it proceeded hand in hand
  with a love of order and legality.[7]

Not a revolution in the utopian expectation of the emancipation of humans from all constraint upon passion and desire, but only the sober and moderate expectation of certain unalienable rights under free government—freedom under law. That the goal of the American Revolution was moderate civil freedom made the struggle revolutionary indeed, but at the same time it is the second cause of that sobriety which distinguishes the American Revolution from the disastrous revolutions of our age and which is our theme tonight.

But what of democracy we must now ask? Perhaps, as I have claimed, the Declaration is neutral regarding democracy, but does the American Revolution not somehow have something to do with the establishment of democracy in this country? It does indeed, and the revolutionary establishment of democratic government in America is at once perhaps the most revolutionary element of the American Revolution, and its most sober aspect.

Americans, Tocqueville observed, were born equal. This was so because of historical reasons too familiar and also too complicated to dwell upon here. The Englishmen who came to this country were from the middling walks of life and the institutions they developed here were far more democratic than those of their contemporaries and kinsmen in England. America, as Marx observed in the same spirit as Tocqueville, did not have a "feudal alp" pressing down upon the brow of the living. During one hundred and seventy years of colonial life the *stuff* of American life was thus quietly being prepared in the direction of democracy. But democratizing as the American colonial experience had been, colonial *thought* on the eve of the Revolution remained essentially pre-democratic. Colonial thought was in unanimous accord with the dominant English and Continental belief in the doctrine of the mixed regime, or, as Englishmen called it, the balanced constitution. This idea, more powerful than ever in eighteenth century England, derived from a two-thousand year tradition stemming from Aristotle. The traditional idea rested upon the premise that the pure forms of government—monarchy, aristocracy, and democracy—all tended to their own corruption; any unchecked ruler, be he the one, the few, or the many, would become tyrannical. Hence, the idea of the mixed or balanced regime—that is, a combination of the three kinds of government in one to prevent that otherwise inevitable degeneration or corruption.

For example, in England this meant the balance of Crown, Lords, and Commons. There was nearly unanimous American agreement on this political prescription, especially on that part of the teaching which emphasized that pure democracy was peculiarly untenable. So great a leader of the American Revolution as John Adams subscribed to the idea of the mixed regime until the Revolution (and in fact never quite rid himself of it). For example, the English constitution, he said, is "the most perfect combination... which finite wisdom has yet contrived...for the preservation of liberty and the production of happiness."[8] It cannot be stated too emphatically how strong a hold this mixed regime concept had on all colonial thought up to the eve of the Revolution.

But the American Revolution changed all this and therein lay its profoundly revolutionary character. As Tocqueville said, when the American Revolution broke out, "the dogma of the sovereignty of the people came out from the township and took possession of the government."[9] The essentially popular character of American life was quickened by all the forces of the Revolution. The logic of the struggle against royal and aristocratic England tilted the Americans more wholly toward democracy. The flight of propertied Tories had the same effect. The old colonial institutions of government, always predominantly popular, became still more so with the removal of royal governors and councils. Democracy became the dominant fact of the new American confederation of states. The Americans found themselves becoming democratic without having intended to become so, an apparently healthy way to ease gently into democracy.

Once independence was declared, each of the colonies was obliged to flesh out its existing institutions and assume full responsibility for its own governance. Each of these new state governments was more fully democratic than its colonial predecessor. But in almost all of them there were also significant vestiges, and perhaps more than vestiges, of the powerful old mixed regime idea. Thus wealth, for example, was given a privileged standing in many of the state governments. Suffrage qualifications differed for the different state offices, like the popular house, upper house, and governor; more property was required for the right of voting for the higher offices. And even more dramatically there were steep property requirements for office holding, the higher the office, the steeper the requirement.

These oligarchic elements in the state governments testified powerfully to the force of the old idea of England's balanced constitution. Thus, democratic as had been the pace of events during the Revolution, there still was the possibility that in time the democratic tide would recede, that property and privilege would reassert their perennial claims, especially perhaps in the South. Or perhaps, say, in Massachusetts in the aftermath of a struggle like the Shays' Rebellion. Whatever might have been the course of events, however differently things might have developed in each state and region, the massive and dramatic fact is that the issue of democracy was settled in this country by the drafting and ratification of the Constitution.

For example, with one single and little remarked clause of the Constitution, those vestiges of oligarchic privilege in the states, those live remnants of the mixed regime idea, were forever barred and the idea of democracy rendered legally complete in the American system. I refer to Article I, Section 2, which establishes the then broadest possible democratic franchise as the basis for the federal election. There was no practical possibility thereafter, under the Constitution, for the gradual reintroduction of aristocracy, wealth, or privilege into the federal suffrage—and if not in the federal suffrage, then inevitably, in time, also not in the state suffrages. To this may be added the total absence of any property qualifications, contrary to existing state practices, for any federal office, and also the clause barring the introduction of any titles of nobility. Finally, we may note the provision for the payment of salaries to federal officeholders, thereby insuring that men of relatively humble means could afford to serve the government.

These quiet and usually unremarked clauses of the Constitution are part of the means by which the Constitution completed the most dramatic aspect of the American Revolution—namely, the firm establishment of the democratic form of government. With the Constitution the Americans completed the half-revolution begun in 1776 and became the first modern people fully to confront the issue of democracy. But, again, the American Revolution precisely in its revolutionary thrust was simultaneously distinctively sober. The way the Constitution confronted democracy is the third and most important element in the "revolution of sober expectations" that we have been discussing.

The sobriety lies in the Founding Fathers' coolheaded and cautious acceptance of democracy. Perhaps not a single American voice was raised in unqualified, doctrinaire praise of democracy. On the contrary, there was universal recognition of the problematic character of democracy, a concern for its weaknesses and a fear of its dangers. The debate in American life during the founding decade gradually became a debate over how to create a decent democratic regime. Contrary to our too complacent modern perspective regarding democracy, which assumes that a government cannot be decent unless democratic, our Founding Fathers more skeptically, sensibly, and soberly, were concerned how to make this new government *decent even though democratic.* All the American revolutionaries, whether they were partisans of the theory that democratic republics had to be small or agrarian or only loosely confederated in order to remain free, or whether they retained the traditional idea that democracy had to be counterbalanced by nobility or wealth, or whether they subscribed to the large-republic theory implicit in the new Constitution — all the American revolutionaries knew that democracy was a problem in need of constant solution, in constant need of moderation, in constant need of institutions and measures to mitigate its defects and guard against its dangers.

It was in this sober spirit that the American Revolution cheerfully and cannily worked its way out of the eighteenth century into the era of modern democracy. The half-revolution begun in 1776 reached its completion only when the peculiar American posture toward democracy received its definitive form in the framing and ratification of the Constitution a decade later. Nothing, then, is more instructive for modern Americans who wish to understand the genesis and the genius of the institutions under which they live than the debates of the Federal Convention of 1787 — that second event which hallowed this hall. And in contemplating that convention we would find the answer to our earlier question: how did our institutions spring from the Declaration and what had to be added to bring those institutions into being? They sprang on the one hand from the love of free government inspired by the noble *sentiments* of Jefferson's Declaration, and on the other hand from the theoretic *wisdom* of James Madison whose sober clarity regarding democracy gave the shape and thrust to our unique democratic form of government and way of life.

The way was opened for the quiet and mild genius of Madison to gain its ascendancy by a stroke of fortune that could lead one almost to attribute the success of the Constitutional Convention to the direct intervention of Divine Providence—namely, that during the summer of the convention John Adams happened to be in London and Thomas Jefferson in Paris serving their country as ambassadors. Had these two formidable figures—the one a lingering partisan of the mixed regime, the other too easily given to a mere libertarianism that would have vitiated the effectiveness of government—had Adams and Jefferson been in Philadelphia in 1787, I do not believe that the single clear vision of Madison would have been able to prevail. And had not Madison and his great colleagues, Washington, Hamilton, Wilson, Morris and the others, prevailed, had not the Constitution prevailed, the half-revolution so brightly begun in 1776 would have had a far less successful outcome, indeed, perhaps a variety of disastrous outcomes.

Tocqueville who understood us so well understood that what distinguished the American Revolution was its successful ascent to the Constitution.

If ever there was a short moment
when America did rise to that climax of glory
where the proud imagination of her inhabitants
would constantly like us to see her,
it was at that supreme crisis
when the national authority had in some sort
abdicated its dominion.

At precisely that moment of crisis when other revolutions turn turbulent, begin to devour their own, and dash all the initial hopes, at precisely that moment ripe for disaster, the American Revolution achieved its glory by a unique moment of stillness and sobriety.

That which is new in the history of societies
is to see a great people,
warned by its lawgivers
that the wheels of government are stopping,
turn its attention on itself without haste or fear,
sound the depth of the ill,
and then wait for two years to find the remedy at leisure,
and then finally,
when the remedy has been indicated,
submit to it voluntarily
without its costing humanity
a single tear or drop of blood.[10]

Only a "revolution of sober expectations" could have brought itself to successful completion in such a moment of stillness. And we have been celebrating tonight the causes of the sobriety that made that moment and that completion possible.

IV On this approaching bicentennium of the Revolution,
I have tried to turn our attention to the two founding
documents of our national being — the Declaration
of Independence and the Constitution — and I have
tried to make it impossible for us to think of the one
without simultaneously thinking of the other. In this
I have followed but also reversed the magisterial
effort of Lincoln. He devoted himself to drawing
the Americans of his generation back from the
Constitution to the Declaration. He did so because
Americans then were emptying the Constitution of
its inspiriting love of equal freedom for all. In the
interests of slavery or of compromising with slavery,
Americans of his generation were reducing and
corrupting the Constitution to a mere legalistic
compact emptied of the abstract truth which it had
once embodied, and which had made it a promise and
a model to all men. When the men of his day spoke
of the Constitution, he wished them always to think
also of the Declaration and hence of the liberty
in which the nation had been conceived and of
the proposition regarding equality to which it had
been dedicated.

Today our needs are otherwise. Our two documents must as always be seen as indissolubly linked. But now we need to train ourselves, when hearing the Declaration's heady rhetoric of revolution and freedom or when it is foolishly cited as authority for populistic passions, always soberly to see the Constitution as the necessary forming, constraining, and sustaining system of government that made our revolution a blessing to mankind and not a curse. In an age of rising expectations, unbridled, utopian expectations, nothing could be more useful than to look back to the sources of the sobriety that spared us in our birth the disasters of revolution which have befallen so many others.

I have not spoken tonight to any of the grave contemporary issues that tear at us and surfeit us with apparently endless crisis. But whatever we each think must be done to solve this or that problem, I call on you here to take your guidance and bearing from that double star of undiminished magnitude — the Declaration and the Constitution — which in two great exertions of political sentiment and intellect burst forth from this place.

Footnotes

1   Roy P. Basler, editor,
    Collected Works of Abraham Lincoln
    (New Brunswick, N.J.: Rutgers University Press, 1953)
    volume 4, page 240.

2   Emphasis supplied by lecturer on following words:
    sentiments; so far as I have been able to draw them; feeling.

3   James Madison to Thomas Jefferson, February 8, 1825,
    in *The Writings of James Madison,* edited by Gaillard Hunt
    (New York: G. P. Putnam's Sons, 1900)
    volume 9, pages 218-19.

4   Letter of April 6, 1859,
    in *Collected Works of Abraham Lincoln,*
    volume 3, page 376.

5   *The Federalist,* Number 14, edited by Clinton Rossiter
    (New York: Mentor Books, 1961), page 104.

6   Gertrude Himmelfarb, *Lord Acton*
    (London: Routledge & Kegan Paul, 1952), page 141.

7   *Democracy in America,* translated by G. Lawrence
    (New York: Harper & Row, 1966), page 64.

8   Quoted in Bernard Bailyn,
    The Ideological Origins of the American Revolution
    (Cambridge: Harvard University Press, 1967), page 67.

9   *Democracy in America,* page 52.

10 Ibidem, page 102.

The American Revolution: Three Views

Freedom In A Revolutionary Economy

Common Ram.

OVIS.

Ewe.

Plate CCCLXX.

Ewe.

Iceland Ram.

Spanish Ram.

Barbary Wedder.

Morvant of China.

Broad tailed Sheep.

Indian Ram.

Ram of Tunis.

Cape Sheep.

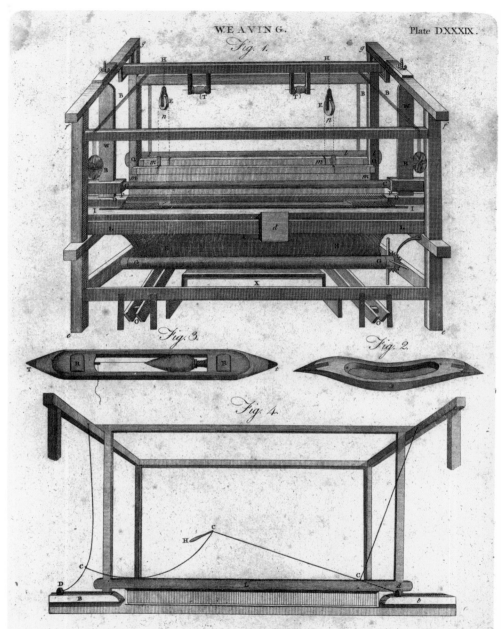

Fig. 1.

Fig. 3.

Fig. 2.

Fig. 4.

A. Bell Prin. Wal. Sculptor fecit.

III
Freedom In
A Revolutionary Economy
By G. Warren Nutter

I   Times change. When my townsman, Thomas
Jefferson, journeyed to Williamsburg in May 1779
and shortly afterward took up residence in the palace
as governor, Virginia was at war. Strange things were
happening in the economy, and they were to become
stranger over the ensuing two years of Jefferson's
stewardship. Inflation was rampant, goods were
requisitioned, property was impressed, salt rationed,
hoarding declared a crime, and exports put under
embargo. Short of arms, Virginia launched an abortive
project to produce them in a state arsenal. If price and
wage controls were not widely or vigorously applied,
it was in spite of constant urgings by the desperate
Continental Congress to do so. The lessons of
experience were simply too compelling: wherever and
whenever price and wage fixing had been tried in the
new states fighting for independence, it had brought
nothing but great economic mischief.

As we assemble here today in Williamsburg on the eve
of the bicentenary of our republic, we may be grateful
for one important difference in the times: we are
not now at war. In that respect, times have changed.

This is not to say that the harsh measures resorted to in the revolutionary war were normal for the colonial period as well. Quite the contrary. Under the British policy of "salutary neglect," in force until 1763, the colonial economy had been largely spared the mercantilist imprint of the age. "Plenty of good land, and liberty to manage their own affairs their own way," Adam Smith observed, "seem to be the two great causes of the prosperity of all new colonies." But why, he wondered, had progress been so much more rapid in the English colonies of North America than in other European colonies throughout the world? The answer was not to be found, he thought, in a richer or more abundant soil, but rather in institutions that enabled the English colonists to make better use of the plentiful resources at their disposal.

These were, first, political. As Smith put it, "in every thing, except their foreign trade, the liberty of the English colonists to manage their own affairs their own way is complete. It is in every respect equal to that of their fellow citizens at home, and is secured in the same manner, by an assembly of the representatives of the people, who claim the sole right of imposing taxes for the support of the colony government."

But there was more. Plenty of good land meant not only abundant resources but also, in a less literal sense, the elbow room needed by a new social order if it was to discard those vestigial institutions that had stifled progress for so long under the established order of things. A case in point was land tenure itself, which could be freed from the bonds of primogeniture and entail in the absence of an entrenched nobility or similar aristocracy. The new society could, when permitted by the mother country, strike out in new directions and prosper accordingly.

The contribution of the mother country was,
in Adam Smith's eyes, strictly that of a mother:

In what way, therefore,
has the policy of Europe contributed
either to the first establishment,
or to the present grandeur of the colonies of America?
In one way, and in one way only,
it has contributed a good deal.
Magna virûm Mater!
It bred and formed the men who were capable
of atchieving (sic) such great actions,
and of laying the foundation of so great an empire;
and there is no other quarter of the world
of which the policy is capable of forming,
or has actually and in fact formed such men.
The colonies owe to the policy of Europe
the education and great views
of their active and enterprising founders;
and some of the greatest and most important of them,
so far as concern their internal government,
owe it to scarce anything else.

The cultural flow did not, of course, cease with the
founding of the colonies. The book from which I have
quoted[1] — *The Wealth of Nations* — was, for one thing,
published the same year as the Declaration of
Independence. And then there was James Watt's
invention of the steam engine scarcely a decade
before. This remarkable confluence of ideas laid the
foundation for a revolutionary society. All at once, it
seems, there sprang forth this congenial triad: a novel
concept of representative government, a science of
economics, and an industrial technology, each
revolutionary in its own right and exponentially so
when combined together.

These ideas had their proximate origin in two amazingly small circles of minds, one located in the incipient United States and the other in Scotland. Though no Virginian can gladly resist the temptation to do so, I will not dwell on the American circle, so well known to us as our Founding Fathers. And, as far as the Scottish circle is concerned, the only point I wish to make here is that Smith and Watt were once colleagues at the University of Glasgow.

John Rae, Smith's biographer,
describes their relation in this way:

There is nothing in the University minutes
to connect Smith in any more special way
than the other professors
with the University's timely hospitality to James Watt;
but as that act was a direct protest
on behalf of industrial liberty
against the tyrannical spirit of the trade guilds
so strongly condemned in the Wealth of Nations,
it is at least interesting
to remember that Smith had a part in it.
Watt, it may be recollected,
was then a lad of twenty,
who had come back from London to Glasgow
to set up as mathematical instrument maker,
but though there was no other
mathematical instrument maker in the city,
the corporation of hammermen
refused to permit his settlement
because he was not the son or son-in-law of a burgess,
and had not served his apprenticeship
to the craft within the burgh.

But in those days of privilege
the universities also had their privileges.
The professors of Glasgow
enjoyed an absolute and independent authority
over the area within college bounds,
and they defeated the oppression of Watt
by making him mathematical instrument maker
to the University,
and giving him a room in the College buildings
for his workshop
and another at the College gates
for the sale of his instruments.
In these proceedings
Smith joined, and joined, we may be sure,
with the warmest approval....

Watt's workshop was a favourite resort of Smith's
during his residence at Glasgow College,
for Watt's conversation, young though he was,
was fresh and original,
and had great attractions
for the stronger spirits about him.
Watt on his side
retained always the deepest respect for Smith,
and when he was amusing
the leisure of his old age in 1809
with his new invention of the sculpture machine,
and presenting his works to his friends
as "the productions of a young artist
just entering his eighty-third year,"
one of the first works he executed with the machine
was a small head of Adam Smith in ivory.[2]

Respect for Smith was hardly confined to Watt or Scotland, for *The Wealth of Nations* migrated easily and widely abroad, finding an eager audience in many parts and certainly on our shores. Our Founders were familiar with this great work in one way or another, some more than others.[3] Alexander Hamilton, Tench Coxe, or whoever wrote the renowned *Report on Manufactures*, paraphrased Smith at length and quoted him verbatim at one point, though without acknowledging the source.[4] Deliberations at the Constitutional Convention reveal a much wider group acquainted with the emerging science of economics.

Passage of time has caused differing verdicts to be rendered on the originality, rigor, and consistency of Smith's masterpiece, but history leaves no doubt about its massive impact and significance. Its genius derived from the molding together of fragments of evolving economic thought into a synthetic whole, masterfully applied to familiar situations in a way that revealed a coherent system for organizing social activity not easily envisaged before and destined to capture the imagination of thoughtful leaders ready to grasp revolutionary ideas. It, like the Declaration and the ensuing Constitution, struck a spark in receptive tinder. Social thought was not to be the same afterward as before.

Ideas do have consequences, dependent on the historical conjuncture into which they are thrust, and this was a propitious time for exciting ideas. The political thinkers and leaders who arose in those formative years of our republic were, of course, influenced by many things: vested interests and personal ambition as well as idealism and ideology; conventional wisdom and prevailing institutions as well as radical thought; the sheer momentum of affairs as well as rational calculus. So was the electorate whose consent was sought and needed to launch the new society. Those who easily discern a simple order in history, an uncomplicated nexus of cause and consequence, may single out one or another factor as the dominant force shaping the course of events in those times, but not I. Such sweeping interpretations of history obscure more than they reveal. Opportunities and constraints are the stuff of history, together with chance, reflective thought, and choice. And none of these elements flows mechanically and predictably from the nature of man, custom, institutions, or any other readily identifiable single source. History is instead the product of all these interacting forces mutually influencing each other. My only object, then, is to give revolutionary ideas and sober reflection their due in this singular epoch.

When the delegates assembled for the Constitutional Convention, there was good reason in circumstances of the time for their attention to be drawn to the related issues of strengthening government at the national level and of "regulating commerce," a term that had roughly the same meaning then as "economic policy" has today. Prosperity had not spontaneously emerged in the wake of independence, contrary to great expectations before the fact. Instead of prosperity, there was depression, aggravated in no small measure by the confused and confounded government of the Confederation. Experience in dealing with these troubles was modest from all points of view: influential leaders were in their thirties; conscious economic policy on the part of government — in London as well as at home — had a history of scarcely more than a score of years; and precedents for the envisaged new order were lacking altogether. Imagination and vision were bound to assume commanding importance.

Wherever and however they acquired their economic vision, the makers of the Constitution deliberately gave wide berth to the economy of the nation being formed, reserving only a restrained guiding hand for government. In saying this, I am mindful of the persistent controversy over how much power the prevailing constitution-makers intended to bestow upon the government of the Union. On this score, however, I find quite persuasive the case made by William Grampp,[5] eminent historian of economic liberalism.

Concentrating on the eleventh-hour efforts at
the Convention to expand the economic role of the
federal government, Grampp notes that

What is interesting is that the proposals —
all of them controversial, almost provocative —
should have been made
only a few days before the convention adjourned,
when unanimity was urgently needed
and when many delegates were trying heroically
to find compromises that would produce it.
Proposals such as that made by Madison
(to empower the Federal government to charter corporations)
had been made earlier in the convention.
That they were made again
so near the time (of) adjournment
suggests that their advocates
were making a last great effort
to write broad economic powers into the Constitution....
Perhaps they prevailed upon Franklin
in the belief
that his great authority would be decisive.
But they were defeated....
The very extensive powers proposed
by Randolph, Morris, Franklin, Hamilton, and Madison
were reduced to the limited provisions
of Section 8 of Article I,
which include the power
to tax, borrow, regulate commerce,
pass uniform bankruptcy laws, coin money,
establish post offices and post roads,
and grant patents.

The limits thus established take on significance
when compared with the traditional economic powers
of the age, which, as Grampp observes,

can be deduced from the controls
which the governments of France and England
exercised or tried to exercise
during the period of mercantilism,
from the sixteenth
to the middle of the eighteenth century:
the fixing of prices, wages, and interest rates,
prohibitions of forestalling and engrossing,
regulating the quality of goods,
licensing of labor,
programs to increase the population,
sumptuary control, monopoly grants
and other exclusive rights,
incorporation, state enterprise,
and the control of foreign trade and finance
including the protection of domestic industries.
The convention considered only four:
monopoly and other exclusive rights,
control of foreign trade, state enterprise,
and sumptuary control.
The last two were rejected.
The granting of monopoly rights
was restricted to patents and copyrights.
The control over foreign trade
was left in an ambiguous state,
except for the prohibition of export taxes.
Although not made explicit,
the Constitution allowed some power
to increase the population,
because the Federal government
could offer free land
as an inducement to immigration.

Good often issues more from powers denied to
government than from those granted, and this was
surely the case as far as economic development over
our republic's first century is concerned. None of the
prohibitory provisions of the Constitution was to take
on greater significance than the one forbidding
individual states to erect barriers to commerce among
themselves. Making trade free within an internal
market that was to expand to vast proportions
permitted the nation to indulge, for example, in
recurrently restrictive tariffs, as the politics of a good
century and a half seemed to dictate, without serious
hindrance to economic progress. Our great market
was to lie at home in a free-trade area larger than
the world has yet experienced anywhere else.
Our Founders could hardly have foreseen that this
would happen, but they must have had a conceptual
vision—no matter how crude it might seem to
those passing judgment today—of the broad benefits
that would ensue from internal free trade.
Otherwise, why bother to write this strict prohibition
into the Constitution?

While such specific sentiments of the time are rather easily discerned, the underlying social philosophy is more elusive, defying simple description in the ideological vocabulary of today. Liberalism will hardly do as a description if only because slavery was accepted by most and extolled by many. Nor can we speak of a democratic ideal in the modern sense, since democracy — either as then comprehended or as since manifested — was specifically rejected in favor of republicanism, a quite different concept of representative government as Irving Kristol so elegantly clarified earlier in this series. Individualism is perhaps the term that best captures the essential spirit of the time and at once implies the complex of derivative values: liberty for the citizen — which is to say, the person deemed competent and responsible — to make his own decisions; power for the citizen, mainly in the form of private property, to realize his potential; humanitarian concern for the less fortunate and incompetent; and equality of all citizens before the law and of the electorate within the polity.

II If the thinker-turned-statesman had his moment
at the founding of the republic, it was to be the
practitioner pure and simple — the doer, the man of
action — who was to dominate the scene for at least the
next century, when pragmatism became America's
watchword. The individualistic spirit found
expression in the world of affairs, not in philosophic
reflection, as each citizen was swept up in the
excitement of his workaday world — his farm or
business, his trade or profession, his public or private
life. The nation, it would seem, was too busy enjoying
the fruits of progress to ponder its causes, and theory
emerged from practice. Political thought issued
from practicing politicians, and economic thought —
interestingly — from practicing jurists.

Economists, such as there were, were either special
pleaders or academic amateurs. In his classic essay on
early American economic thought, the late Frank
Fetter wondered "why...the fertile and original
conceptions which sprang, as it were, spontaneously
from the new environment in America, [did] not
come to fruition in a constructive and more lasting
system of American economic thought."

He found much of the answer to lie in "partisanship, which blocks the path of disinterested scientific effort whenever personal prejudices and pecuniary or class interests are affected by the application of any kind of theory to practical problems."

The consequence—and, in turn, reinforcing cause—was lack of a learned profession of economics. As Fetter observes:

It is a remarkable fact
that during the whole period before 1870
there was not a single so-called political economist
who had received
the minimum amount of special training
demanded today for the practice of law,
or of medicine,
or for the pursuit of the natural sciences.
All were trained primarily
in some other field:
theology, moral philosophy,
literature, languages,
law, practical politics,
journalism, business,
or some branch of natural science.
In political economy
they were all self-trained amateurs,
who, as it were,
happened to wander into this field.
If the study of the more exact sciences
were pursued only
by men with such dominant motives
and such unspecialized training,
little scientific progress could be expected.[6]

I leave it to others to judge whether the absence of trained economists made us better or worse off in this first century of sweeping economic development. However that may be, the fact is that there was no body of qualified scholars, skilled in critical thought, to observe the unfolding economy, issue commentary, formulate general principles, apply them to problems of the time, and advise on policy. Instead it was the law, issuing from acts and cases, that was to shape a framework for the economy, articulate its principles, and guide policy.

The propelling legal philosophy of the era conceived the purpose of law to be, in Roscoe Pound's words, "a making possible of the maximum of individual free self-assertion." Or, as James Willard Hurst has put it more concretely:

We continually experienced
the tangible accomplishments
of individuals, small groups, and local effort,
with a heady sense of living in a fluid society
in which all about him all the time
one saw men moving to new positions
of accomplishment and influence.
Our background and experience in this country
taught faith in the capacities
of the productive talent residing in people.
The obvious precept
was to see that this energy was released
for its maximum creative expression.[7]

At the same time, those who made and interpreted the law were not slaves to some sterile dogma of laissez-faire. Far from it. As Hurst reminds us, this was no "Golden Age in which our ancestors — sturdier than we—got along well enough if the legislature provided schools, the sheriff ran down horse thieves, the court tried farmers' title disputes, and otherwise the law left men to take care of themselves." There was no reluctance to legislate positively "where legal regulation or compulsion might promote the greater release of individual or group energies."

But the pervasive spirit of the law, whether it invoked or restrained the power of government, was individualistic. It was normal that "the years 1800-1875 where, then, above all else, the years of contract in our law."[8] Subject to the restrictive doctrines of consideration and residual authority of the state to refuse enforcement, the thrust of the law was to encourage voluntary exchange and association. The legal system was responding to the burgeoning scope of the market and in turn stimulating further expansion, in a process of interaction similarly experienced in England at an accelerating pace during the eighteenth as well as the nineteenth century.

It was, in fact, an English jurist who, with typical facility, gave classic expression to the legal philosophy dominant in our first century:

If there is one thing more than any other
which public policy requires,
it is that men of full age and competent understanding
shall have the utmost liberty of contracting,
and that contracts,
when entered into freely and voluntarily,
shall be held good
and shall be enforced by courts of justice.[9]

In a word, contract was king, a sovereign precept demanding obedience from subservient legal principles. No wonder the courts and legislatures were so busy elaborating and defining property rights and liabilities, sweeping away vestigial restrictions on alienation, erecting an intricate structure of commercial law, and creating the corporate person with its full range of appendages and paraphernalia.

The spirit of the time may be fairly interpreted as enthusiasm for venture, viewed as the source of prosperity and progress. Consequently, the law leaned over backward not to hinder the entrepreneur, not to hold him unduly responsible for incidental harm flowing from venturesome activity. It was as if "nothing ventured, nothing gained" had become the literal creed of the age.

For, as Hurst points out,

The insistence on a showing of criminal intention
(in any case involving liability)
amounted in effect
to a presumption in favor
of the independence of individual action.
The middle-nineteenth-century rationale
of the law of negligence, in tort,
reflected the same basic value judgment.
Expansion of economic energies brought men
into closer, more continuous relations
in situations increasingly likely to yield harm.
Nonetheless, at first
the law emphasized the social desirability
of free individual action and decision.
Liability in tort
should normally rest on a showing of fault
on the actor's part;
action at one's peril was the exception.
Hence the burden lay on the injured person
to show reason
why the law should intrude its force
to shift some of the burden of loss
onto the one who caused injury.[10]

This attitude no doubt appears strange to a generation accustomed to the rhetoric of Ralph Nader and the Sierra Club. I have dwelt on these legal presumptions of the last century neither to extoll nor to disparage them, but to stress their importance as a manifestation of the social ethic of the time. Who is to bear the burden of proving what, and why? The presumptive answers given to these questions say more about a society's conception of the good life than any list of good intentions, no matter how long.

In the matter-of-fact world of our first century, freedom took on concrete meaning in the market-place, and it worked. A continent was settled, a nation built, and prosperity persistently augmented. The portentous questions of slavery and preservation of the Union might overhang the political scene, but the grand passion was economic development, and the object of the love affair was the market, the creature of free enterprise and exchange.

III So it was at least on the surface, but something
happened on the way to our second century.
There was, first, the torment of the Civil War, which
probably served more to arouse the social conscience
than to soothe it. Yet, the slaves freed and the Union
preserved, the economy hardly paused before
plunging into the era of bigness, surely the
culmination of a less abrupt historical process.

What had been happening on the economic front was
a revolution in transport, the spanning of the
continent by railroad, creating a truly national market
and opening the way for big business, big finance,
and all the other forms of bigness. The individualistic
spirit was bound to be put under severe stress as
gigantic voluntary associations, the very creatures of
contract, assumed a corporate and depersonalized
nature basically in conflict with the principle of free
individual choice.

Tocqueville had already been impressed in the 1830s by the remarkable ability of American private enterprise to mobilize large sums for grand ventures, but he noted that "what most astonishes me is not so much the marvelous grandeur of some undertakings as the innumerable multitude of small ones."[11] Now grandeur was to take the center of the stage.

It is neither my bent nor purpose to prolong this historical narrative, for the moment will shortly be upon me for a summing up, and there is more interpretive ground yet to be covered. Suffice it to say that our first century laid the basis for the second, still fresh in memory. We gradually moved toward a turning point similar to the one faced earlier in England. As Winston Churchill was to write at the turn of the twentieth century,

The great victories had been won.
All sorts of lumbering tyrannies had been toppled over.
Authority was everywhere broken.
Slaves were free.
Conscience was free.
Trade was free.
But hunger and squalor and cold were also free
and the people demanded
something more than liberty....
And how to fill the void
was the riddle that split the Liberal party.[12]

Changing opinion ultimately brought forth a second revolution, a revolution in social thought born of economic crisis some two-score years ago. In the formative years, we seemed determined to make up for lost time in the realm of social philosophizing. The vanguard of social reformers comprised a multiplying band of intellectuals, spawned by affluence, emboldened by their own peculiar sense of superiority, motivated by the animus of the onlooking outsider, and hence, as Schumpeter perceived, inherently inclined to become angry social critics by profession. Learned economists, conspicuously absent during our first century, appeared in abundance and assumed a role of growing importance. To be sure, ardent defenders of the free society were to be found in the intellectual ranks, particularly among economists, but they were vastly overshadowed by the critics in due course. The way was prepared for the sharp inversion of social values that has taken place over the last generation, an inversion incarnate in the colossal government that has come into being as the share of the nation's net product passing through the hands of government has risen from less than a sixth to more than two-fifths. Security, protection, comfort, equality—all seem to have advanced in the scale of importance above self-reliance and freedom.

Fundamentally, what has been transformed is the prevailing conception of the good society. In the nineteenth century, it was the way of life that was idealized—the process whereby the achievable was to be achieved. Today, it is the achievement itself, the outcome of the process, that is prized. We value the way of life less and the content more.

Why has this happened? The easy answer is that freedom did not live up to promise. The evolution of legal principles during our first century suggests that freedom was valued in the economic sphere for what it was expected to yield, that its worth was deemed to be instrumental rather than intrinsic, that economic progress was the goal and freedom merely the means.

There are two things to be said about this interpretation. First, by the test of progress, freedom can hardly have been judged a failure. Production, despite periodic bad times, moved upward in a trend that was the envy of the world, while population multiplied fifteen-fold.[13] This was, after all, the "land of opportunity."

Second, freedom was surely desired for itself as much as for its consequences. To interpret the moving spirit of our founding years as nothing more than a craving for greater material comfort would be a travesty of history. Not even the sustained paralysis on the slavery issue can lead us to a similar conclusion about the succeeding period. Nor do we need to become mired in the metaphysical to define liberty as it was then conceived. The documents of our Revolution protested against too much government, against the dead hand of paternalism and arbitrary power. Liberty to our Founders meant freedom from government.

Perhaps, then, Marx was right in proclaiming that the benefits of capitalism would be far outweighed by its evils: increasing monopoly, misery, inequality, and insecurity. Here, too, the evidence argues otherwise in the main.

Of course, poverty did not vanish amidst plenty, but in a broader sense there was no discernible worsening of material inequality during our first century. A recent study shows, for example, that slaveholding, then unfortunately an important aspect of wealth, was no more concentrated in 1860 than in 1790: in both years, the top one percent of slaveholders owned about an eighth of the slaves. Better and more direct evidence indicates a small but perceptible reduction in the inequality of incomes during the last four decades of the nineteenth century.[14]

Changing circumstances and lack of records make it impossible to assess the trend of monopoly in the nineteenth century. Seemingly obvious appearances can be deceptive: the era of trusts toward the end of the century accompanied the emergence of a national market and hence did not necessarily signify a decline of competition. Those who envisage an earlier age of more pervasive competition in isolated localities are likely to be indulging in myth. In any case, the evidence for the twentieth century has been carefully sifted, and it shows no upward drift in the extent of monopoly.[15]

To give Marx his due, one must acknowledge that, over most of our history, we were plagued by cycles of boom and bust with intensifying social impact, so that the attendant insecurity and periodic unemployment constituted a major source of discontent and ultimately of social crisis. But recurrent depressions are not enough to account for the profound change in social outlook.

Instead, I would argue, success has had more to do with our changing mentality than failure. It was Mark Twain who said: "If you pick up a starving dog and make him prosperous, he will not bite you. This is the principal difference between a dog and a man." Progress did not, by and large, aggravate inequities, but it made us more aware and less tolerant of them. Sharpening contrasts in circumstance aroused our humane sentiments, sentiments that could be better afforded by virtue of augmenting affluence. Progress shook loose the age-old endurance that man had customarily displayed for his lot, and bred in its place an attitude of insatiable discontent with the pace at which remaining problems were being met. And so we find ourselves in a society in which progress and discontent are engaged in an almost desperate race with each other.

This is perhaps as it should be as long as there is poverty and injustice in the midst of plenty. If social change is to move in the right direction, in accord with the standards of the civilized world, there must be those who stir and prod, who keep the public alert to inequities, who find fault with the established ways of maintaining social order. It is natural to point the finger of blame at the existing system and to seek salvation in its opposite, but therein also lies the great danger of our day.

Those who protest against failures of the market, real and imagined, too often see their remedy in turning affairs over to government, in expanding the political order and diminishing the economic — in relying more on coercion and less on mutual consent. The danger we run in looking first to government to solve problems is that progress will grind to a halt — that discontent will vanquish progress, and the race will be over. Over the ages, the bane of progress has been too much government, not too little.

IV The time has therefore come, as we approach our bicentenary, to look back to the origins of our economy and to reflect on where we go from here. The revolutionary content of ideas popularized by Adam Smith and implemented by our Founders is to be found in the vision of a complex social order organized not by custom and command, the methods of the ages, but by voluntary exchange and association. Economics arose as a scientific discipline when the economy became a social order distinct from the polity. Those who, inspired by the spirit of freedom, sought to broaden the individual's control over his own destiny were naturally inclined to enlarge the scope of markets and to reduce that of the body politic. The economy became an area of social activity coordinated through voluntary agreement, and economic activity became in the main synonymous with liberty.

Progress came with the loosening of political bonds, but the resulting freedom could be translated into action only through power. The individual acquires power through ownership of private property, the other side of the coin to liberty. In the absolute state, subjects enjoy neither freedom nor power: the despot reigns over slaves. By becoming concentrated in his hands, private property ceases to exist in any meaningful sense. Put the other way around, private property is the means whereby power may be dispersed within a society. It is no wonder that our legal system devoted so much attention to strengthening and vitalizing this institution.

The opposite of the absolute state is anarchy, where everything is privately owned. Just as there can be no freedom in the absolute state, so there can be no order in anarchy — and hence no freedom either. On this earth, there must always be collective property embodied in the power of even the freest state and accumulated through the instrument of taxation, itself an inherent property right of every state. It is equally clear that a society becomes free and democratic only as property becomes broadly dispersed and predominately private.

Over most of our history, the question of what middle ground was to be occupied by our society between the poles of anarchy and despotism was resolved by the presumption that matters are best left to individual choice and mutual consent unless the contrary is proved beyond reasonable doubt. The burden of proof was upon him who maintained that a task entrusted to the market could be better performed by transferring it to the government.

The state had much to do, but classical liberalism implied a certain ordering of tasks to guide the emphasis of governmental activity. First, the state had to provide the necessary political and legal framework for the market by maintaining order, defining property, preventing fraud, enforcing contracts, and assigning responsibility. Second, it should disperse power by diminishing inequality of income and opportunity and by inhibiting monopolization. Third, it was to perform desirable functions too costly for individuals or voluntary associations, such as establishment of a sound monetary system, maintenance of public health, and promotion of safety. Fourth, it should help the poor and unfortunate and act as guardian for the incompetent, protecting those who could not cope with the normal responsibilities of life. Fifth, it should stabilize general economic conditions. Sixth and finally, it should provide welfare services to the public in the form of social security, unemployment assistance, and various other desired collective goods.

That ordering has been turned upside down by the social outlook of today, and the shifting emphasis has caused government to undertake the activist role formerly assumed by the market. That is, the ascendant presumption is that matters are better attended to by government than by the market. Wherever performance of the market is under attack, those who believe that government would do an even worse job bear the burden of proof.

This state of affairs obviously accords with the prevailing vision of the good life. And so one might conclude that there is nothing more to be said, since the people have the social order they want. But do they?

One may be permitted to wonder whether there is not some profound confusion in a society that strives so hard to retain a peacetime economy through seven long years of war and then leaps into a wartime economy almost the moment peace breaks out. More fundamentally, something must be wrong in a society that feels compelled to treat each new problem, no matter how routine, as a monumental crisis and hence chooses to live in a continual atmosphere of tension, sacrifice, and fear. As a friend of mine has put it, if the price system is not to be trusted with adjusting a 20-percent gap between the supply and demand for energy, perhaps it had better hang up its spikes.

But I am here today to note the trend of affairs, not to pass judgment or to prophesy the ultimate outcome. Who can see what will come in the next two centuries any more clearly than our forefathers could envisage what vast change lay ahead in the two just completed? In a way, our starting point is similar to theirs. Recall the traditional mercantilist controls of central government rejected by our Founders: the fixing of prices, wages, and interest rates; the outlawing of forestalling and engrossing; the regulating of the quality of goods; the licensing of labor; the setting of sumptuary standards; the granting of monopoly rights; the chartering of corporations; and the establishing of state enterprises. They have all found a congenial home in the New Deals, Fair Deals, New Frontiers, Great Societies, and New Federalisms of our age. Yet, the very environment being created by them affords us something to react against in the same way that our forefathers did, perhaps once again to the benefit of liberty. As the saying goes, good judgment comes from experience, and experience comes from bad judgment.

Let me then end on a soft note of hope in keeping with the occasion. My mood is unfortunately one of hope rather than expectation, for there is little in the momentum of unfolding history to comfort those who cherish freedom. What is there to prevent the fraction of income taxed by government from rising to half, three-quarters, and more? There is a hope, and it is this: having become so impressed with the fact that freedom is not everything or the only thing, perhaps we shall put that discovery behind us and comprehend, before it is too late, that without freedom all else is nothing.

Footnotes

1   Adam Smith, *The Wealth of Nations*
    (New York: Modern Library, 1937)
    pages 538, 551 and 556.

2   John Rae, *Life of Adam Smith*
    (New York: Augustus M. Kelley, 1965)
    pages 73-74.

3   See William D. Grampp, *Economic Liberalism*
    (New York: Random House, 1965)
    volume 1, pages 128 and following pages and 154.

4   See Edward G. Bourne,"Alexander Hamilton and Adam Smith,"
    Quarterly Journal of Economics,
    volume 7 (1893-94), pages 328-344.

5   Grampp, *Economic Liberalism,*
    pages 101-114.

6   Frank A. Fetter,
    "The Early History of Political Economy in the United States,"
    in James A. Gherity, editor,
    Economic Thought: A Historical Anthology
    (New York: Random House, 1965)
    pages 489 and following.

7   James Willard Hurst,
    *Law and the Conditions of Freedom
    in the Nineteenth Century United States*
    (Madison, Wisconsin: The University of Wisconsin Press, 1956)
    Page 7.

Footnotes

8   Ibidem, page 18.

9   Sir George Jessel, cited in Ibidem, page 12.

10   Ibidem, page 19.

11   Alexis de Tocqueville, *Democracy in America*
(New York: Vintage Books, 1954)
volume 2, page 166.

12   Winston S. Churchill, *Lord Randolph Churchill*
(New York: Macmillan Co., 1906)
volume 1, page 269.

13   See L.E. Davis, R. A. Easterlin, W. W. Parker, and others,
American Economic Growth:
An Economist's History of the United States
(New York: Harper and Row, 1972)
pages 21-26, and 33-50.

14   See Ibidem, pages 29-32 and 50-54;
and Lee Soltow,
"Economic Inequality in the United States
in the Period from 1790 to 1860,"
Journal of Economic History
(December 1971), pages 822-839.

15   See G. W. Nutter and H. A. Einhorn,
Enterprise Monopoly in the United States: 1899-1958
(New York: Columbia University Press, 1969).

Publisher

American Brands, Inc.,
is a manufacturer of consumer products.
Its oldest brand, Jim Beam Bourbon, dates from 1795.
Its Lucky Strike brand dates from 1856.
The company also makes Pall Mall,
Tareyton, Silva Thins, Carlton cigarettes and
Half and Half smoking tobacco.
Other products based on American agriculture include
Sunshine Biscuits crackers and snacks
and Duffy-Mott apple and prune products.
The American Cigar Division makes
La Corona, Antonio y Cleopatra and Roi-Tan cigars.
Swingline staplers and Master Lock padlocks
are leaders in their respective fields,
as is the Wilson Jones name in office supplies.
Acme Visible Records produces
business forms and information systems.
Other well-known American brand names include
Jergens and Woodbury lotions and soaps.
American Brands also operates in Great Britain
through ownership of Gallaher Limited,
a large tobacco company founded in 1857
which is today a diversified consumer goods company

Colophon

This edition of
The American Revolution: Three Views
is published by
American Brands, Inc.
The illustrations are from
Encyclopaedia Britannica, 1797.
The type face is Baskerville.
Printing and binding are by
Kingsport Press,
with photographic copy by
The Meriden Gravure Company.
Design of the book is by
Bradbury Thompson.
January 1975